Shadc

By Beryl Anthony Brackett

Lyfe Publishing

Publishers Since 2012

Published by Lyfe Publishing LLC

Lyfe Publishing
10800 Nautica Place
White Plains MD 20695

Library of Congress Cataloging in
Publications Data

Beryl Anthony Brackett

Shadows of Strength / Beryl Anthony
Brackett

ISBN: 978-1-7349079-2-6

(Fictitious Character)-Fiction

Washington, DC

Shadows of Strength–Fiction

Printed in the United States of America

1 2 3 4 5 6 7 8 9 10

Book design by Olivia Pro Designs and Lyfe
Designs

Editor

Ryan Brackett

BAB Reviews

18103 Merino Drive

Accokeek, MD 20607

DEDICATION

In celebration of a friendship that has spanned decades. To Olivia, my friend in laughter and reflection. You're not just a friend, you are family. We didn't know we would have similar experiences, but here we are. I dedicate this book to you. Although this a story of fiction, I see you in every page I turn. You are resilient. You are strong. You are courageous. You are my friend.

ACKNOWLEDGEMENT

God, you are AMAZING! I thank you for how you have kept me through the years. There is none like you. Without you, I wouldn't be here! For that, I am truly grateful! Thank you for your healing, for your love, for your grace and mercy!

I would like to thank my family for always supporting me in everything that I do. A huge thank you to my husband Taurus Brackett, Sr. I am so grateful for your love and support. My editor, Ryan Brackett, who always makes sure that my writing says exactly what my heart feels. Thank you!

To all my beta readers, thank you for taking time out of your busy schedule to read my draft and give your honest feedback. Juanita M. Smallwood, when I asked you to read my manuscript, you did not hesitate. Not only did you not hesitate, you also read it within a day. For that, I am grateful. Your feedback and suggestions were priceless!

Avis Dillard, I so appreciate you. I appreciate you taking the time to read Shadows of Strength. Thank you for your feedback and your attention to detail. Thank you, you rock!

Dawn Atkinson, a huge thank you for providing character insights to help the story move forward. Your comments did not go unnoticed. Thank you for being a part of this journey with me. I am very grateful!

To Lyfe Publishing, thank you Gerald C. Anderson Sr., for your support and for helping me stay focused. I'm still learning to make a list and check it off to complete the task at hand. I have you to thank for that! Now my list is checked off and the task is completed. Thank you for everything!

Also, By Beryl Anthony Brackett

Missing Daddy

The Leah Grace Series

Broken Pieces

Breast Cancer Healing Scriptures Guided
Journal

1 – In the Beginning

Twenty years ago.

Karrington Lewis entered her high school year on top of the world. Touting a 3.8 grade point average from middle school and honors society recognition, everyone believed she would be successful in life. The first two years were just that… amazing. She sat in the band and worked with various clubs. Her teachers were honored to have her in their class.

One day during Karrington's junior year, she arrived at school with a worried heart. She sat in her history class hating it. History was one of the required classes. It wasn't fun. She enjoyed the classes that challenged her mind, like chemistry, trigonometry, and physics. She also enjoyed the fact that most jocks like Rich Johnson were not in those classes. Rich sat next to her in this class. He always annoyed her.

During her history class, Rich, the quarterback of the football team, leaned over and whispered in her ear, "You're too pretty to have a long face. How about we fix that?"

She smiled, not wanting to hurt his feeling. "I don't think so. Everyone knows you and Diedre are going together." She smiled that 'I don't think so,' smile at him. "I'll pass."

Rich nodded, like he had it under control. "Me and Diedre broke up a few days ago."

"And you're already after me?" Her face frowned, hoping to send the don't play me signal that would end this conversation.

"We officially broke up a few days ago. It was over long before that."

Mr. Baker chimed in, "Maybe Rich would like to tell us what's so important that he can't pay attention."

Rich laughed. "No sir, I'd rather not say anything."

Mr. Baker replied, "Then I suggest you look this way and pay attention. Your GPA could use a boost." The class broke out in laughter. "I don't know why some of you are laughing. You're in the same boat as Mr. Johnson here."

Rich responded, "Sir, people like me don't need this class. What am I going to do with history in the NFL? I'm going to be making millions and throwing touchdowns for a living." Most of the class chuckled. Everyone knew Rich was big in football. One player high fived with him. "I'm only in this class because I need it to graduate. I don't need it where I'm going."

"What if you don't make the NFL? Do you know how many high school football players there are in your class across the country? Do you know how many actually make the NFL? Son, you would do yourself good if you focused on your education to have something to fall back on." Rich didn't respond. Karrington looked at him. She lived two doors down from Rich, so she heard the fights at home. She knew Rich's dream of the NFL was a reason to get away from home. He hated his life there, but he believed it was the only way for him. Mr. Baker continued, "Mr. Johnson… Rich, and all of you athletes in this class, don't put all your eggs in one basket. Use sports to get you a good degree so you will have the means to support yourself without sports."

Mr. Baker's face stiffened, "I knew a guy who was just like you in high school. Everyone celebrated him. I believe he had over 70 offers from schools across the country. Many believe he would easily make the NFL. Although, he got to college, he realized the game was faster than he expected. Many of the players were simply better than he was. In the end, he got scouted by the Miami Dolphins. However, he never made the team. The smaller the pool of players there are, the harder it is to make the team. If I were any of you, I would use my talent to get a good degree. That way, you have something to fall back on." The bell rang and everyone jumped up to leave. "Don't forget the test tomorrow. It counts as a third of your grade."

Karrington felt bad for Rich. "Hey, it may sound harsh, but he's got a point. You'll get into a great school. Get your education and play football. If you get into the NFL great, but just in case you don't, you will have the tools to make a great living."

"Can I walk you to class?"

Karrington wished she had left well enough alone. She didn't want to say no, and she didn't want to say yes either. "Okay." *Darn it. Why couldn't I be tough?*

"You know, playing football is the only thing that frees me from my troubles. I'm sure you heard all the fights at my house." Karrington didn't want to answer, so she listened. "Everyone on the street hears them. My family is so dysfunctional. When I'm on the field, I block all of that out. It's just me and the game."

"That's okay. Just remember education is important, too."

"I'm not as smart as you, Karrington."

"Studying… I study a lot."

"Can I come study for the test tomorrow?" She looked away, hoping something would come up. "I could use the help, Karrington. No one in my family is smart."

Her grandmother raised her to be a helpful person, so she couldn't say no. "Okay, but it's just to study Rich."

"I totally understand. I'll be there at 7, after football practice."

"Okay." She stopped. "This is my class. Thank you for walking me."

"You're welcome. I'll see you tonight."

She smiled and walked into the classroom. Karrington took her seat. Chemistry was her favorite class. One day, she wanted to be a doctor or a pharmacist. Moments after she took her seat, Diedre walked into the class. She sat two aisles away from Karrington. Diedre placed her books on her desk, then made a beeline toward Karrington. *Oh boy, here we go.*

"Did you think I wouldn't notice you and Rich?"

"I didn't think about it at all."

"So you're after my man?"

"I'm not. Rich had a tough time in class, so we walked and talked about it. Anyway, he said you broke up with him."

"We break up to get back together all the time." Diedre headed back to her desk. "Stay away from him."

I knew I should have said no. This was the last class of the day, and Karrington couldn't wait to get home. Diedre followed her to the bus. She realized Diedre wanted to make sure she stayed away from Rich. What she didn't understand was that Karrington didn't want Rich. She never had a boyfriend before, but she knew the person she wanted would not be an athlete. Karrington wanted a man who was smart. She craved intelligent conversation with her man. She had no desire for sports, except to watch her baby brother, Jalen play baseball.

Once on the bus, she was happy. Diedre went the other way, and now she could relax on the ride home. The tap on her window scared her. It was Rich. *Oh my God, really.* She let down her window not to be rude. "Hey Rich."

"Hey, they canceled football practice. Do you want a ride home?"

"No thanks. I've had enough of Diedre for one day."

"Diedre? I told you we broke up."

"Tell her that." Karrington sat down and waved goodbye to him. Rich frowned and headed to the parking lot. *I really hope he doesn't show up to study.* Karrington arrived home as usual. There were cars in front of the house. *Hmm, I didn't know everyone was coming over today.* She walked into the house. The faces of her aunts and uncles were grim. She didn't like what she saw. That feeling in the pit of her stomach that she felt when she was eight years old returned. She asked, "Where's grandma?"

Aunt Lisa said, "Momma is in the room resting. The doctors told her she has cancer."

"Oh no." Karrington slumped down on the couch. She understood what cancer meant. It took her mother and now it was coming for her grandmother.

Aunt Lisa sat beside her, "You know your mother was a fighter. She got it from your grandmother. This isn't over by a long shot. Don't give up hope."

Her words were touching, but the downfall of studying to be in the medical field was knowing that death can't be defeated, and cancer was one demonic evil that took her family members away. She heard her brother call out to her. "Karrington, grandma wants you."

Karrington stood up and walked to her grandmother's bedroom. Grandma had ten children, and Karrington hated walking past each one of them. Grandma was strong, although she was in her 80s. Realistically, she didn't have a lot of time, but Karrington wanted each second she could get. They were all precious to her and she wouldn't be deprived of them.

She walked into Grandma's room. And was met with a smile. It also changed Karrington's emotional state. Instead of depression, she suddenly switched to joy. Grandma had that way about her. Grandma said, "Honey, come here and give me a hug."

Karrington followed her instructions. "Hey grandma. I heard what the doctor said."

"Honey, never give up. God is the one we need to listen to and until He says it's time, I will be here living my life and working for the Lord."

"Amen, grandma!" Karrington was more enthusiastic than ever. Her grandma wasn't giving up, and neither would she. Karrington hugged her again. "I love you Grandma!"

"I love you too, honey."

Karrington bounced out of the room. Aunt Lisa said, "There's a young man here to see you."

Karrington's happiness dissipated. Her prayer that Rich would not show up was not answered. She deeply sighed and headed to the front of the house. She looked at Rich, wondering how this was going to go down. "Hi Rich, now is not a good time."

"I know. Your aunt told me. I just wanted to say, I'm sorry. I know what you went through with your mom." Rich continued, "I'm also sorry for Diedre. She's being a jerk, so I will back off until all of this clears."

The response surprised Karrington. She didn't think Rich knew the first thing about being a responsible person. She looked at him differently now. "Thanks Rich. I appreciate your kind words. I hope everything works out for you and Diedre."

"In all honesty, I don't. She's changed over the last two years, so I know I need to move on. There's no sense in getting involved with anyone else right now, so I'll just get myself together."

His words truly blew Karrington away. She couldn't believe Rich was so mature. *Someone must have coached him.* "Again, thank you Rich." He turned and walked out of the house. Karrington's aunts and uncles were giggling at her. She was embarrassed. Karrington put her hand over her face and walked into her room.

The Next Day

Karrington woke up. She wanted to check on her grandmother before she got dressed. Jalen ate cereal at the table. "You should be headed out the door."

"I will."

Karrington walked into the room. Her grandmother was awake and sitting on the bed. "Hey Karrington. Help me get dressed, honey. I have to go to the doctor. Your Aunt Lisa is coming to pick me up."

"Okay grandma." While Karrington helped her get dressed her admiration grew even more. Grandma shared stories with Karrington that amazed her about her family's strength. She knew she had the strength to fight and one day that strength would be tested.

Grandma said, "Honey, I know you're not old enough to remember, but this isn't your grandma's first bout with cancer. I've rung that bell two times already. I plan to do it again."

"Wow, Grandma, I didn't realize that."

"Yeah honey, the first time was scary, but I wasn't giving up. I fought for five years before I won and rang that bell like crazy. The last time, I fought for two years and won again. I don't know what will happen this time, Karrington, but I want you to know cancer is a vicious enemy of the Lewis family. If it comes to you... fight it, honey! Fight it with everything you got!"

"I will, Grandma." Karrington got dressed for school. Aunt Lisa picked up her mother and took her to her appointment. At school, Karrington couldn't help but think about her grandmother. She loved her so much. After her mother died, her grandmother took them in and raised them. Her aunts and uncles all chipped in as well, but it was her grandmother that helped to get them through the hard time. It was especially hard on Jalen since he was younger.

The bell rang for lunch. Karrington could never bring herself to eat the school's lunch. She thought it was horrible. There was a burger joint next door she went to sometimes. This would be one of those days. Her friend Olivia joined her. "Hey Karrington."

"Hey Olivia. How's your morning going?"

"Rough girl. That trig test was a beast, but I'm sure you aced it."

"I doubt it. My mind has been on other things."

"Come on Karrington. Grandma Lewis is a fighter. She's not going anywhere."

"You know, I think it's easier for the one fighting than the ones watching the fight."

"You're probably right. Hey there's your boy, and he's with Diedre. He lied to you."

Karrington frowned, "Why am I not surprised? All that mess he said yesterday was just a load of crap."

Olivia shook her head, "Or she just has that power over him. You know some dudes can't get enough. When you turned him down, he ran right back to her."

"That's a possibility, but who knows and frankly, I've got bigger things to worry about."

"Yeah, like should you get a single or a triple!"

They both chuckled, knowing Karrington would never eat a triple burger. Olivia always tried to get her to try something new, but she always went back to her single with fries. The two of them ordered their food before the crowd converged on the joint. They mostly sat in silence, staring at the classmates, who were laughing and talking. Rich looked at

11

Karrington, but Diedre pushed his face back at her. Karrington and Olivia snickers. Karrington said, "You're right, she has him under her control."

"I told you."

They got up and returned to school. Karrington attended her advanced English class while Olivia had concert band. Karrington sat in class wondering how her grandmother was doing. It didn't take long to find out. A student walked in with a pink slip. Karrington never got called to the office, so she paid it no attention until the teacher called her name. Karrington thought it was a mistake and didn't move. The teacher said again, "Karrington! You're wanted in the office."

Karrington got up. Her spirit felt numb. She suspected God was preparing her spirit for bad news. Karrington tried to brush it off, but it wouldn't go away. She slowly walked to the office where Aunt Lisa met her. Now she knew it was bad news. Her aunt only came to her school once before, the day her mother passed. Karrington whispered, *"Not again."*

The Gravesite

Karrington cried her eyes out at the gravesite. Many of her classmates joined her at the funeral. She was thankful for that. She wondered how many more times she would have to stand at a gravesite for someone she loved. Her family was big, so she reasoned it would be several. After the funeral, Rich came up to her. "Hi Karrington. I'm so sorry for your loss. I heard your grandmother was a fighter. I always admired her."

"Thank you, Rich. It took cancer three times to get her. I admire her strength and courage."

"Yeah. I know it's hard on you. If you want to talk someday, let me know."

She smiled and tilted her head, "Are we doing this again, Rich? We both know Diedre is not going for it. I wish you guys the best." She tapped him on the shoulder and walked away. She rejoined her family and grieved with them.

2 – Law School Graduation

Eight years after the passing of her grandmother, Karrington walked across the stage at Georgetown University. She was excited to start her career in law. Aunt Lisa said, "Karrington, I didn't believe you when you said you were giving up medical school for law school, but you're so smart you can do anything you like."

"After so much death in my early years, I couldn't help but let it go. I can't be a doctor and watch more people wilt away. I'm excited though. This lawyer thing is good. I get to argue my point more times than not."

"Well, I'm excited for you. Everyone is waiting at the house for your big celebration."

"I'm on my way. Olivia is coming too."

"Great! Did she go to law school?"

"No, she's a captain in the Air Force now. She came home on leave to watch me graduate."

"Awesome. See you both at the house."

Karrington hugged her aunt. She turned to find her friends. In the distance, she spotted Olivia. They made their way to each other. Karrington congratulated her classmates as they congratulated her. She finally made it to Olivia. "Girl, it's a lot of people here to see you graduate."

Karrington laughed, "I don't think they're all here to see me." The friends laughed and hugged each other. Karrington and Olivia hadn't seen each other since they graduated college together. After college, Olivia received her commission in the Air Force. They sent her to Germany for three years. "So, how's life at Andrews?"

"It's cool. I'm on the fast track to become a major. The wing commander seems to have taken a liking to what I bring to the table."

"Great! I'm so happy for you."

"How about you? Any job offers?"

"Yes, I have several. I'm sifting through them now. It's not easy trying to decide who to go with."

"I bet it's not. That movie about the law firm in Louisiana comes to mind. You know, the one where they turned out to be working for the mob."

"Oh yeah, no girl, I can't be doing that."

"I know that's right. You should look into being a lawyer for the Air Force."

"No, I can't do that either. My place is right here in DC. I want to fight for those who can't fight for themselves. I'm thinking about joining the public defender's office, but I'm not sure if that is he right move for me."

"That's not much money."

"I know, nevertheless it will give me experience so I can open my own law firm in the future. You know, stop working for the man!"

"I know that's right, but the Air Force could use good lawyers like you. What about a reserve officer?"

"I'll think about it." Karrington wasn't going to think about it. She wanted to move from the conversation. She had no intention of joining the military. Karrington said, "Hey, let's grab some coffee before we head to the party."

"Sounds good to me."

They arrived at their favorite bistro in Washington, DC. Karrington ordered an espresso while Olivia ordered a chai latte. They sat outside to enjoy the pleasant breeze. They made small talk until Olivia's mouth dropped. Karrington asked, "What's up?"

"Look."

Karrington looked behind her. Her eyes widened, "Rich, how are you?"

"I'm doing well, Karrington. Hi Olivia."

"Hi Rich, it's good to see you."

"It's good to see both of you." He smiled. "May I sit?"

Karrington said, "Sure, have a seat."

"I haven't seen you guys in what, seven years? Wow, time flies."

"It sure does," Olivia said. "What have you been up to?"

"Well, I didn't get into the NFL as I once dreamed of doing but thanks to Karrington, I have a great job in IT." Karrington twisted her head in a tell more way. "Remember the conversation we had in history about my education and the NFL?"

"I do." She snickered.

"Why you laugh like that?"

"I just dreamed of you saying that in front of a pastor."

Karrington's eyes popped again, "Diedre?"

"She's long since been out of the picture."

Olivia said, "Do tell."

"Well, as you know, the summer after high school me and Diedre got married. It was good for a while. After I blew out my knee in my junior year, she saw no hope of me getting to the NFL. She started having an affair with the guy who replaced me and now they're married. He's in the NFL but not starting."

"I'm so sorry to hear that," Karrington responded. She's wrong for that. You don't leave someone when they're down. That's the time you stick with them the most."

17

Olivia added, "I agree with you, Karrington. Karma will come back to her for that."

"I was bummed out for a while, but I kept remembering what Karrington and Mr. Baker told me. 'Don't put all your eggs in one basket', he would always say. He was right. You both were right, Karrington." Karrington rubbed his shoulder. He was different now. Not the brash young man who thought the world owed him something because he could throw a football. This Rich was different. He is mild mannered and caring. "Anyway, I got heavy into the books. Because of football and partying, I was behind in my studies. I caught up and graduated last year." Karrington and Olivia clapped. "With a 3.5 at that."

Karrington smiled, "Awesome, Rich. I'm so happy for you. What did you major in?"

"Engineering. I'm a biomedical engineer."

"Outstanding," shouted Olivia. "I'm impressed."

"So am I. This guy got Ds in history class. Rich, you've come a long way, dude."

Rich smiled and dropped his head in a shy manner, "Yeah, I never believed in myself until I only had myself to count on. I watched my father deteriorate in front of my eyes. Before that, he beat my mother so many times she can't remember who she is. I vowed I would never watch anyone suffer like that again, so I design software programs that test new drug therapies."

Karrington shook her head, "I am utterly amazed, Rich. I'm also very happy for you. Football isn't everything. What you have will last you forever."

"Yeah, but I would give anything to be out there throwing the ball around again. I love the sport. I thought about coaching a pee wee team."

Olivia said, "Do it. There's nothing that can stop you."

He nodded, "I will. Next season I will sign up for a team in my neighborhood."

"Awesome", said Karrington. "Hey look, we have to be going to my aunt's house. They're having a party for me."

"Oh, it's your birthday?"

"No, I just graduated from law school."

"Law school? You were going to be a doctor."

"Yeah, like you I also got tired of watching people deteriorate so I became a lawyer instead. I couldn't handle it anymore."

"Understood. Enjoy your party."

Olivia motioned to Karrington. She knew what she was trying to say, but she wanted to ignore it. She gave in. "Rich, would you like to follow us to the party?"

"Sure. I have nothing to do. Thanks!" Rich excitedly said. Clearly, he was hoping to be invited.

Karrington fought off the desire to frown. Instead, she forced a smile onto her face. She liked the apparent new version of Rich but questioned if it was real or not. Karrington had seen him pretend to be something he was not before. She wondered if the years made a difference to him. She would watch and see. Karrington and Olivia reached her car. Karrington pulled out into the street and Rich pulled in behind her. They were off to her aunt's house.

Olivia said, "He's changed."

"I don't know Olivia. I've seen this side of Rich before. Pretending and all."

"Yeah, but something is different. Then again, something is the same."

"What does that mean?"

"He still carries that torch for you. He always did like you."

"Lust… it's something totally different."

"No, I think he genuinely likes you."

Karrington heard her words. She wasn't buying it. Rich always appeared to be a genuine person, but then the other side of him comes out. She wondered if they could be a couple. After her focus rested on school for so many years, it was nice to think about having a relationship. "If he is a genuine date this time, it would be nice to only see that side of him. You know how he was in high school. Almost caused a fight between me and Diedre. You know I'm no fighter."

"I know that. Smart as heck, but can't fight a lick."

They both laughed. Karrington pulled up to the house, and they got out. Rich was behind them and got out of his car. There were several cars parked around the house. Karrington's little cousins ran up to her and gave her a hug. "Hey guys, I'm a lawyer now."

"Karrington, you're smart," one of them said. "Is that your boyfriend?"

"No honey, just a friend." Rich joined them. "Welcome to my Aunt Lisa's abode. Come on inside and meet everyone." Karrington led Rich inside the house while Olivia played with the kids. Inside, Karrington introduced Rich to her family members. The men were watching baseball while the women were talking. "Hey is Jalen playing?"

"No, this is the majors. He plays tonight," her uncle answered.

"Okay, my brother is going to the majors one day." She turned to Rich. "Jalen got drafted by the Orioles in the minor league. However, he hasn't been called up yet. He makes a decent salary playing in the minors, though."

"That's awesome. He was always good."

"Yeah, I'm the brains and he's the brawn." They chuckled. Karrington led him to the sunroom. She often liked to sit back there and think about her life. Losing her mother, never knowing her father, and then losing her grandmother was hard on her. If it wasn't for her aunts and uncles, she would have fallen apart. She motioned for Rich to take a seat and she did the same. "So, tell me about your life now."

"My life is much better now. After me and Diedre broke up, I focused on getting my degree. I got this job and I'm good at it. I have an apartment in Northeast, so I'm doing well."

"Both your parents are gone?"

"My dad died but my mom is alive. She suffers from memory loss. My dad beat her so much she's nothing like she used to be."

"I'm sorry Rich. I know I heard shouting and arguing a lot from your house. I used to pray for all of you."

"I guess it didn't work."

"It worked for you." He smiled. "You seem to be a better person today than you were in high school."

"Thanks, but my life didn't work out."

"Maybe it did Rich. Everyone wasn't made for the NFL. You're doing some good stuff in the job you're in now. God has a plan, and you are doing what he wants you to do."

"While Diedre married an NFL player like she wanted."

"You can't focus on her. She will get hers." He held his head down. "You can't keep looking at the downside of things. You have a lot of positives in your life right now."

"You're probably right. I just feel used by her. She never loved me, she only loved what she thought I could do for her. In the long run, I'm probably better off."

She patted him on the shoulder, "You are better off. People who want you for what you can do for them aren't worth your time." She nodded, "Let's talk about something else."

"What do you want to talk about?"

"I have no idea." They both laughed. "So, who's this company you work for?"

"Dobb Industries. They are a highly rated Fortune 500 company. I was lucky—"

"Blessed."

He snickered, "I was blessed to get with them. Hey, you like dressing up and going to dinner parties?"

"Hmm, let me think. The last one I went to was… never." They doubled over in laughter. "I'm a college graduate without a job right now. So where would I go to a dinner party, Rich?"

He continued to laugh, "I guess you're right." He stared at her, giving her the feeling that he was truly falling for her. Something inside her made her realize this time it was real. He meant it and there was no game being played. "Will you go to my company's dinner party tomorrow night?"

"Sure, I have nothing planned."

"Great. I'll pick you up at six."

"Sounds like a plan."

He stood up, preparing to leave. "This will be our first date. I'm excited."

"So am I Rich." She smiled and grabbed his arm. This was real to her now. The boy she felt annoyed by in high school was winning her heart. He wasn't the brash football player anymore. He was a smart man, the man who could steal her heart. She walked him to the door. "Thanks for coming to my party."

"Thank you for the invite. I'll see you tomorrow."

She wondered if he would kiss her. She thought he might peck her on the cheek at least, but she wasn't sure if she would let him. His eyes asked if it was okay, and she gave him a look that welcomed his next move. He leaned over to peck her on the lips.

Karrington was shocked she didn't resist. For the first time in her life, she wanted it.

"Good night Karrington."

With her eyes still closed, "Good night, Rich." He walked away. Her eyes followed him to the car and watched him drive away. She didn't know how long she had stood there before Olivia arrived.

"Hey Karrington," Olivia said in a teasing tone.

Karrington tilted her head and rolled her eyes. "Don't start."

"I saw that kiss girl. Oh… my… goodness… you guys are going to do the nasty!"

"Stop it." Karrington pushed Olivia away but smiled through it all. She wondered what her first time would be like. She was so enamored with school and getting her education that she never had time for a relationship or sex. Now she was faced with the decision to wait until she was married. Either follow the advice of her grandmother and aunts or ignore them and go all the way. She remembered her grandmother always preached to her about that. What would she do?

3 – The Romance Begins

Karrington spent all day getting her hair done and picking out the right dress. The first dress she picked out, Olivia said, was awful. It hurt Karrington's feelings because she thought it was one of her best dresses. The next one she picked out they both liked. However, she didn't know if it worked for a dinner party at this level. Aunt Lisa walked in and Karrington asked her, "Auntie, is this dress good for the dinner party tonight?"

Aunt Lisa rolled her eyes at the dress and each of them. Karrington knew what the response would be. If anything was true about her aunt, her love for clothes was it. "Are you kidding me? Is that the best you have?"

Feeling embarrassed, Karrington answered, "Yes." Her voice was meek, as though she really didn't want to respond, but it was her aunt and she had to say something.

"Let's go."

"Where are we going?"

"Shopping." Aunt Lisa stopped suddenly and turned, "No niece of mine is going out to a Fortune 500 company looking like a… like she doesn't fit in there."

"Yes ma'am."

26

"I'm going to teach you a few things before you go tonight. I should have done this years ago. You'll need the crash course now. We only have six hours before that boy gets here." Karrington looked at Olivia. Karrington felt Olivia was stunned by Aunt Lisa's words, too. Aunt Lisa continued, "You're coming too Olivia, just in case you need some training. You're part of this family, too."

"Yes ma'am."

No one dared challenge Aunt Lisa. She meant what she said, and she pulled no punches saying it. They got into her car and headed to the store.

After two hours of looking through dresses, Karrington found the one they all agreed would be the one to stun everyone at the dinner. It popped on her. She was never one to show any cleavage or her body, but Aunt Lisa insisted on giving the old white men something to look at. When Karrington resisted to show more cleavage than she wanted to, Aunt Lisa said, "You never know when one of them will want a lawyer. They will remember you when they do." Karrington didn't appreciate using her body in this way. She didn't believe she had a model body until she saw herself in the dress. Most of her attire would just cover her body. Except for Rich, men wouldn't look twice at her. Tonight she felt they would look not only twice, but several times.

They returned home. Karrington, with Aunt Lisa and Olivia's help, got dressed. When they were finished, Karrington looked in the mirror. She was amazed at herself. "Wow, is this a trick or something? Do I really look like this?"

"You never put much into getting dressed," replied Olivia. "All you cared about was those books. Now it's time to wow this man off his feet."

Rich pulled in front of the house. Karrington's nerves increased. She felt a pit in her stomach. It was something she felt when she had a speech to give in class. This was ten times stronger. Olivia touched her on the shoulder. "You might want to go outside. It's the only way you can get in the car." Aunt Lisa and Olivia laughed. "Go ahead, girl. You can do this."

Okay, all I need to do is put one foot in front of the other one. I can do this. She looked at each of them. "I don't know if I'm afraid of going on a date with Rich or going to this dinner party."

Olivia said, "Just go, girl. Everything will work itself out."

"Okay. Wish me luck, guys."

Aunt Lisa said, "We don't believe in luck in this house. Go with God's blessings!"

Karrington smiled, "Thanks Aunt Lisa." She walked out of the house to a waiting Rich. When he saw her, he stood straight up and adjusted his suit. Karrington knew she got his attention. He rushed to her and took her by the arm, guiding her down the steps and to the car. For once in her life, she felt like the queen, the center of everyone's attention. Neighbors watched outside. Some made sweet comments to her and smiled and acknowledged them. *I'm a movie star or something.* She laughed at her thoughts.

Karrington got comfortable in the car, ensuring her dress was perfect when they got to the party. Rich got in and off they went. He said, "You're easily the most beautiful woman in the world."

Karrington loved the comment, but she didn't believe it. "Thank you for the sweet comment. We both know that isn't true."

"But it is. Beauty is in the eye of the beholder. I say you're beautiful… the most beautiful woman in the world."

Her smile ran deep inside her soul. Karrington wanted to trust Rich. She only remembered the boy she knew in high school. Karrington said, "Rich, I'm liking this new version of you… at least this version of who I think you are. Are you for real this time?"

"I am a different person, Karrington. After Diedre left me, I spent months suffering, asking myself how I was going to survive. I even got to the brink of suicide. Somehow, I pulled myself out of that hole. I decided to better myself with education—an idea I got from you. I also changed the man I was. Today's version of me is the Rich I am today. That young boy in high school doesn't exist anymore."

"Suicide? I'm glad you didn't go down that road, Rich. That's never a good option. Turn to God, He'll help you out in any situation if you just believe in Him."

"I'm not one of those Jesus freaks. Sorry."

"Wow, I guess we have one disagreement." Rich didn't reply. The car pulled up to a big house in Washington, DC. The houses in this area were all in the millions. Karrington was in awe of the beauty. She wondered if a life with Rich would work out despite his disbelief in God. His belief could change if she were in his life. She let those thoughts lie until after the party. The valet opened the door for her, and she stepped out. Rich took her arm, and they headed inside the house.

Inside, Karrington marveled at the décor of the home. Nothing like it compared to any home she had seen. As she stepped further inside the home her senses were immediately met with vibrant colors, wall art and masterfully crafted sculptures. Her life was a lower middle class life. This was the life of the rich and famous. "Wow, Rich, your boss lives here?"

"Yeah, he's a millionaire several times over."

"I can imagine."

Rich stopped in front of an older white couple. The man said, "Rich, it's great to see you. I'm so glad you could make it. This is my wife,

Cassandra." Cassandra nodded and shook Rich's hand. "Who is this young lady?"

Rich turned to Karrington, "This is my date for the evening, Karrington. She just graduated from Georgetown Law."

The man said, "That's outstanding." He reached out his hand, and Karrington shook it. "What are your plans now?"

"I have several opportunities to consider. I'll narrow it down to one in the next few days."

He continued, "If you don't mind me asking, what was your class standing?"

"Harold", said Cassandra, clearly perturbed. "We're not here to talk shop."

"I'm not. I'm just trying to help the young lady." Harold turned and motioned to a man who came in their direction.

Karrington answered Harold's question, "I was in the top ten of my class."

Harold grabbed her by both shoulders. Karrington was a little tense and embarrassed. "Hey Guy, this is Karrington. She just graduated from Georgetown Law in the top ten of her class."

Guy's eyebrow rose, "It's nice to meet you, Karrington. I have an opening at my firm. I would love to sit down and talk to you about it."

Rich leaned over and whispered in her ear, "This is how things get done in the city. Take him up on it."

"I'd be honored."

Guy said, "Great. Here's my card. Call my office on Monday and we'll get you in."

"Thank you."

Guy nodded, then shook hands with Harold. Harold said, "They have the third largest law firm. You would do well to get a foot in the door there."

"Wow, the third largest in DC. That's amazing."

He smiled and looked at Rich, "No sweetie, the third largest in the world."

Karrington resisted dropping her jaw to the ground. She realized she had just agreed to an interview with a world power in the law arena. She looked at Rich and realized her resistance didn't work. Rick lightly touched her jaw, closing her mouth. "I'm sorry Mr. Harold. I'm just amazed at what just happened."

Cassandra stepped in front of Harold. "Don't worry, my dear. You'll get used to it. Now let's go freshen up before Harold brings more business talk to you."

Karrington smiled. "Thank you, Mr. Harold."

"You're welcome, sweetheart."

Karrington looked behind her. Harold patted Rich on the shoulder. He said something to Rich. Rich intently listened. She made a mental note to ask Rich about it later. They arrived in the lady's room. There were several people there. Karrington realized the ladies came there to discuss men, business, and the appearance of other women. Alliances were made and lost in the lady's room. Cassandra turned and asked, "How long have you known Rich?"

"Since we were in high school. He was a year older than me and moved on my street when I was 14. So, all-in-all, nine years. But I haven't seen him in five years."

Cassandra nodded her head. "This world is not for the faint or the weak. Things can change in a millisecond. I brought you in here to teach you a quick lesson. Just because you have that offer for an interview today doesn't mean you get the position tomorrow. Be prepared and ready. Some of these vultures around here will watch you."

"Thanks for the heads up."

Cassandra raised her head. Karrington suspected she didn't know what to make of her. But she could handle anything after what she had been through.

"You seem unfazed by what I said."

"I just don't worry about people and things. What's for me is for me and no one can change that."

"You're a Christian?"

"I am."

"My mother used to talk like that, but I realized it was all talk. She never got anywhere in the world. Honey, if you want to make it in this world, make your own luck."

Karrington smiled and turned slightly. She didn't want Cassandra to see she was irked by her comments. "My aunt says we don't live by luck, we live by faith and my faith... hasn't expired."

"You have a lot to learn, young lady."

"That I do, Miss Cassandra. However, I will still keep my faith no matter what I'm faced with."

Cassandra washed her hands, and Karrington did the same. She expected dinner was about to start and that's why Cassandra came into the bathroom. They dried their hands. Cassandra smiled and said hi to a couple of ladies, while Karrington nodded her head at them. They appeared to respect Cassandra and since Karrington was with her, they respected her too. She wondered what they were saying about her behind her back.

Karrington joined Rich at their table. She leaned over and asked Rich, "Who has a dining room this large in their house?"

"One of the richest men in the world."

"I take it you've been here before."

"I have, and I wanted to make an impression this time. That's why I asked you to join me."

"An impression on me or them?"

"Both." He smiled. She felt the allure of him wanting to kiss her. She prayed he didn't. Karrington wasn't one for public displays of affection. Before anything could happen, someone clanged a glass to get everyone's attention.

As the night wore on, Karrington enjoyed the conversation. The meal wasn't large portions, but what she had tasted better than anything she tasted before. The main menu was beef wellington wrapped in a fluffy pastry shell, along with a salad and a lobster bisque. She made a mental note to thank Aunt Lisa for her quick lesson in etiquette. It came in handy for helping Karrington not look like a fool. The last thing she wanted to do was embarrass Rich. Another point she enjoyed was Rich's behavior. He had changed and for the better. The arrogance was gone. This version truly was a man after her heart. She couldn't let on that she liked him that much.

The evening came to a close. Guy reassured Karrington of their meeting on Monday. He even told her to be at his office at 10 that morning. Karrington wondered if Cassandra put in a good word for her. It didn't matter in the end. Her trust and faith were in God and God alone. If she was meant to have the job, she would get it.

Rich continued to be the unexpected gentleman and opened her door. She stepped in. They enjoyed a pleasant ride back to her aunt's house. Rich asked, "Will I get to see you again?"

"Sure. What do you want to do?"

"I'd like to take you to the movies tomorrow, if you're interested."

"I would love to see that new horror movie."

"That's strange, a Christian wanting to see that movie."

"I have my likes and dislikes. It's just entertainment. I know where my help comes from."

"Understood. I'll check for times and hit you up with a text later tonight."

"Thank you, Rich, and tonight was amazing. I truly enjoyed myself." Rich smiled. "By the way, what did Harold say to you when me and Cassandra walked away?"

"He said you would make a great wife." Karrington's eyes popped open wide. "He also said I shouldn't mess it up."

"Oh wow. I made that kind of impression with him."

"I think he was more impressed with your GPA and class standing than anything else." Karrington nodded her understanding. "But I'm impressed with the entire package."

"Rich, you have changed… but I am still watching. I've known you for a while and forgive me for being careful—"

"Be careful Karrington. I want you to watch because all you'll see is a good man, trying to change the perception of what he used to be. I'm not that guy and I don't care how long it takes to win your heart. I will win it. You'll see."

His words instilled love in her heart. If he truly meant it, she could see herself with him, maybe for the rest of her life. "Then we'll take each day slow. I want you to know I'm not having sex until I'm married. If that's a deal breaker, let me know now."

"It's not. Having sex before marriage got me Diedre. She only wanted me for my career. I want someone who truly wants me."

"Okay. I will see you tomorrow, Rich."

"Are you going to church?"

"I am."

"What church?"

"Greater Mount Calvary on 14th and D street."

"Cool."

"Are you coming?"

"Keep a seat warm for me in case I show up." He smiled and blew her a kiss.

"I will do that." She stepped out of the car. Rich joined her and walked her to the door. The couple embraced and kissed. Karrington found each kiss with Rich to be better than the last one. She wondered if it was her inexperience or if he was truly proving to be the one. That was a question that would take time to answer.

Karrington answered questions from Aunt Lisa and Olivia until two in the morning. Olivia stayed the night because she wanted to hear all the details from the dinner party. Details, Karrington was glad to share. For the first time in her life, she was open to a relationship and oddly enough for her, it was with a man she never expected to be involved with. She laid awake, wondering what their life would be like. *I'm putting the cart before the horse right now. It's okay to imagine the perfect life together, I guess. I wonder if he truly understands my commitment to abstinence before marriage. I hope so. That was one thing my grandmother always wanted from me and I'm going to give it to her. If he can't understand that, then there's no place for us. I guess I'd better go to sleep. It will be time for church before you know it.*

Those last words rang true. Karrington's alarm went off, announcing it was time for her to rise. She bounced up, feeling better than she had in a long time. Olivia said, "Don't we look all pepped up and everything?"

"I must admit, I feel great this morning."

"You're still on a high from last night. That dinner must have been better than you let on."

"Oh, it was nice being in the presence of such powerful people, but the part I liked the most was Rich."

"What?" Olivia held her hand over her mouth in shock. "Say it ain't so."

"It is so, and I'm not afraid to admit that I'm taking a liking to him. I went to sleep with him on my mind and woke up with him on my mind. Hmm, what does that mean?"

"That means you're in love. You can't be there already."

"No, I can't be there yet, but I'm open to it."

"Long as you keep them legs closed. Remember how Rich used to be?"

"I remember, but this Rich is different." She looked at Olivia. She wasn't buying it. "He really is different, Olivia." Olivia tilted her head. Karrington imagined she was having difficulty separating the new Rich from the high school Rich. "Look O, do you trust me?"

"Yes, but you know nothing about the matters of the heart. Give you $E=MC^2$ and you know everything there is. However, love isn't a simple calculation. Rich may have gotten better at his game. That's all I'm saying."

"You may be right, and I've got my guard up. I already explained to him about sex."

"Let me guess. He said he was down without having sex until married."

"Yes."

"Karrington, all men say that in the beginning. Give it a month and he's going to be mad because you haven't done it. If you haven't done it."

"I'm not doing it. I promised my grandmother I wouldn't and I'm not."

"Okay, I really wish you the best. Let's get out of here so we can get a good seat at church."

"Sounds good to me." They headed out the door. Olivia drove them to church. It was the first Sunday, so it was packed in the parking lot. Karrington liked to get there for praise and worship. She enjoyed the music. It got her spirit going. They walked in, and Karrington froze in her tracks. Her eyes popped open. She looked at Olivia.

"If your smile gets any bigger, it will block out the moon."

"Shut up O."

Rich extended his hand, and Karrington walked to it. He stepped back and allowed them to enter the pew. Karrington stood by Rich and savored every moment. *Okay grandma, this man is making it hard on me. I'm feeling some kind of way.* She loved his curly

40

hair. His light skin complexion accented hers. Karrington imagined everyone in the church was in awe of them. She held her head high, believing she met the perfect man.

After church, Karrington ran into Aunt Lisa. "Hey Aunt Lisa. Did you enjoy the service?"

"Girl, you know I did." She looked Rich up and down. "Well, it's nice seeing you here today, young man."

"Yes ma'am."

"Look at you, looking all good." She looked at Karrington and Olivia. "What y'all up to today?"

"I'm headed back to the base. I have to work tonight," answered Olivia.

"Really? Can you tell Uncle Sam to let you stay out a little longer?"

Olivia laughed. "It doesn't work that way, Aunt Lisa."

"Okay, what about you, Karrington?"

Karrington looked at Rich, expecting an answer. None came. "We're supposed to go to the movies today."

"But we need to get something to eat first. That is, if you want to have lunch with me."

Karrington couldn't think of anything else. She didn't want to be out of his presence. *Dang, I'm whipped.* "Sure, I would love to have lunch with you."

"Good, let's all get something to eat. I'm starved."

Karrington snickered. No one wanted to tell Aunt Lisa they wanted to eat alone. She, like Rich, decided to just go with it. Karrington rode with Rich. Once inside the car, they looked at each other and broke out into laughter. Karrington held her hand over her mouth. "I didn't want to say anything to her."

"Hey, I totally understand. Maybe she has her reasons."

"She's scouting you, dude. She wants to know if you're good enough for her little niece."

"Then I'm good with that. I'll show her just like I will show the rest of the world. My heart belongs to you, Karrington."

Again, his words lit up her life. She really wanted this to work. They pulled up to the restaurant and walked inside. Aunt Lisa already had a table for three. Karrington and Rich sat down.

Karrington studied the menu. Everyone ordered and enjoyed their Sunday lunch. Aunt Lisa asked a thousand questions, but Rich was great in his responses. Karrington felt more at ease with him than ever. After dinner, the couple sat in front of Aunt

Lisa's house talking until midnight. Karrington said, "I guess I better go inside. I have a big meeting tomorrow with Guy."

"Yes, you do. I'm sure you will knock him off his feet. You've impressed everyone since I met you."

"Aww thank you Rich."

"Let me walk you to the door."

They got out of the car, and Rich walked her to the door. This time, he embraced her and kissed her squarely on the lips. This kiss was more impressive than before. Their tongues danced in harmony together. The feeling Karrington had inside was stronger than ever. She not only wanted to be with Rich for the moment; she wanted to be with him for a lifetime.

4 – The Nuptials

Six months later, Karrington was the happiest woman in the world. She maintained her relationship with Rich, started her new job in Guy's criminal defense law firm and most of all, she kept to her Christian beliefs. Karrington even watched her fiancée get dipped in the water, making him a saved Saint of God. The wedding day was four days away and she couldn't contain herself. She sprung up from her bed, ready to start her day. It would be the last day of work until she married Rich. She loved the name Karrington Johnson. Rich didn't want her to hyphenate her name. He felt it was straddling the fence. Karrington was okay with that. She came from a long line of women who didn't believe in hyphenating their new last name. She would have to remain Karrington Lewis at work. They encouraged lawyers not to change their name.

Karrington stepped in front of the bathroom mirror and felt a twinge in her chest. She felt her breast. In one area, there was a spot that felt different than before. Rubbery. It felt tiny and hard. Sweat rolled down the side of her face. She gasped for air. *This can't be happening to me.* She called Olivia but didn't get an answer. *Okay, calm down. God didn't give me a spirit of fear. Let me just make an appointment and see what's going on.* Karrington finished dressing and headed to work. When she got to her office, she dialed her doctor's number. It took a few minutes, but Karrington got an appointment with her doctor for the next day. *I can't tell Rich about this until I know for sure. Lord, I can't have cancer. Please don't do this to me.* She took a step and remembered how Jesus cried from the cross. *Lord, in this life or the next, I know you got me.* Karrington threw herself into prayer, then hit the floor running with work. She wanted to ease her mind. Every now and then, the thought of having cancer invaded her spirit. In those moments, she moved to God's word. The feeling went away.

Karrington never stopped working, even for lunch. Her phone vibrated in her pocket, causing her to gasp. She laughed at herself. "This is Karrington."

"Oh, that's how you answer the phone now?"

"Hey O, how are you?"

"I'm good, but what's the deal with this urgent message this morning?"

"I found a rubbery spot on my breast this morning." She took a breath. "I'm praying—"

"Don't go there. Your mother and grandmother were fighters. This isn't happening to you. Don't let me come over there and beat you down."

Karrington chuckled inside. Olivia always knew how to keep her strong. "I guess I won't let that happen." She gathered herself. "Let's meet for dinner."

"I'm down. Our favorite spot?"

"Yes, I'll see you there at six."

"Awesome. See you girl and don't give this another thought. You got this."

Karrington didn't answer. She wanted to believe her best friend. After watching her mother and grandmother fight the battle, she wondered if she could do the same. *I guess I should have stayed in the medical field. Then I would have self-examined and determined by now what's wrong with me.* A tear dropped onto the document she was reading. She caught others as they ran down her face. *I can't let this happen to me. Olivia is right. I am a fighter, and I must stay strong.*

The rest of the day moved quickly for Karrington. She kept her conversations with Rich short. The last thing she wanted was to worry him over what might not turn out to be anything. She gathered her things and headed out the door for dinner with Olivia. Her secretary asked, "Ma'am, is the motion ready to file with the court?"

"Yes Louvenia. You can take it down in the morning. Thank you."

"Thank you and have a great evening and wedding."

Karrington smiled, "Thanks, are you not coming?"

"Oh yes I'll be there, but you'll be too busy, so I wanted to wish you the best now."

"Aww, I'm never that busy. See you Saturday."

"Yes ma'am."

Karrington stepped into the elevator with a co-worker. "So, the big day is Saturday. Are you excited?"

Karrington wondered why anyone would ask that question. Excitement comes with the package. "Of course, I'm excited and a bit nervous."

"My wife was all over the place before our wedding. We got a wedding planner, but she might as well have done it herself."

"Not me. I'm letting the wedding planner do her thing. I have enough to worry about." She stepped out of the elevator. "Have a nice evening."

"You, too."

Karrington made her way to the garage. She arrived at the restaurant before Olivia. She got their favorite seat so they could see everyone as they came in. Karrington and Olivia had a habit for watching people. Since they moved into their twenties, they stopped talking about people, but they still watched them. Karrington ordered their drinks. Olivia walked in a few moments later.

"Hey Karrington." They embraced. "I stopped by my place to change. I didn't want to show up here in uniform."

"I totally understand."

"How are you holding up?"

"I'm good. Sort of." She took a sip of her drink, hoping it would hold back the tears. "I worked my butt off today to block out the thoughts of what might be."

"I see." Olivia took Karrington's hand and bowed her head. "Dear Heavenly Father, thank you for bringing us here on this day. We know that you already know what's wrong with my friend and you've already provided the healing. Father, we know each of us has suffered loss at the hands of the demon, but today Father… today we claim victory over it. It will not harm my sister. No weapon formed against Karrington Lewis soon to be Johnson will prosper. In your wonderful Son Jesus' name, we pray… Amen."

"Amen. Thank you for that, Olivia. I don't know what I'm going to do when the Air Force sends you away from me."

"FaceTime, baby. This is the new age, and we are never too far from each other."

"I know that's right, O." They laughed and joked throughout the meal. Karrington enjoyed the banter with her best friend. Toward the end of dinner, Olivia noticed someone walk into the restaurant. Karrington asked, "O, what's wrong?"

"That man. He was my mother's boyfriend. He stood by her to the end. After her passing, I refused to talk to him. I couldn't bring myself to say anything to him because he reminded me of how hard it was losing my mother to cancer." Olivia rolled her eyes at the man when a lady sat down with him. "It's clear he's moved on with his life."

Karrington grabbed Olivia's hand. "I know O. You are one of the few people that understands how it feels to have a loved one taken from you. But it's been ten years give the man a break. He has the right to move on by now." Olivia continued to stare. "Go over and say something to him. I'm sure he will appreciate it." Olivia looked at her, then back at the man. Karrington took her hand and smiled.

"Okay. I was supposed to be here for you." She gulped her drink down. She sat it gently on the table, half smiled at Karrington, then got up and walked over to the man's table.

Karrington watched as the man's face lit up. He was happy to see Olivia. It brought a smile to Karrington's face as well. She received a text from Rich. He was always sending her a text telling her how much he loved her. She understood that if the test result were positive for cancer, she would have to postpone the wedding. She replied with some cute words and a kissing emoji.

Olivia returned to the table. "Thank you for pushing me over there. It was a friendly conversation. We're having lunch tomorrow. He's retired from the Air Force, so we're eating at the Officer's Club."

Karrington smiled. "That's awesome, O. See, things turn out better than you think they do." Olivia turned her head. "Okay, okay, I need to follow my own advice. I will. My appointment is tomorrow and I'm sure nothing will come of it."

"That's the right thing to say, Karrington. I just hope when you go home tonight that you continue to believe that in your heart." Karrington didn't reply. She knew better than anyone she would think the worst. Having lost her loved ones early in life, it was hard for her not to. "Karrington." Karrington looked down. She felt the water in her eyes roll like an ocean. She hoped she could hold it back. It didn't work. "Karrington honey..." Olivia moved to Karrington's side of the table. She put her arm around Karrington. Karrington couldn't stop the tears from rolling down her face. They were contained for most of the day. Now she couldn't hold it back anymore. Olivia continued to hold her and tell her everything would be okay. It reminded Karrington of the encouragement she provided to her mother and grandmother.

Karrington gathered herself and pulled back. "Thank you, Olivia. I needed that cry."

"We all do at times, girl." The server arrived with their bill. Olivia took it. She searched her purse for her credit card. Karrington did the same. "Put your card away, Karrington. I got this."

"No, you don't need—"

"I got it, girl. Chill." She handed the server the card and bill. "Do you have a military discount?"

"We do." Olivia went to her purse to get her identification. "Don't worry, I believe you." The server walked away. "Karrington, you are my best friend. If you ever need me, please let me know and I'll be there. We have gone through so much together. I will never let you down."

"Thank you, Olivia. I feel the same about you. Now get me to the altar on Saturday."

"Yes, ma'am!" They laughed. Olivia signed the receipt, and they each headed to their cars and home.

When Karrington arrived home, Aunt Lisa was in front of the television yelling at the potential presidential candidates. She was big on politics. Karrington could care less about it. She hugged her aunt and kissed her on the cheek. Karrington wanted to tell her about her doctor's appointment but decided she cried enough for one day.

Once in her room, she flopped on her bed. The act allowed her to release everything. She pretended to see all her worries rise to the top of the ceiling and dissipate. *I wish it was that easy.* She laughed at herself. *I wonder what my man is doing. Well, let's see.* She called Rich, and he picked up immediately. It still amazed her at the differences between Rich in high school and the current Rich. "Hey babe, how are you?"

"I'm good. We are just sitting around planning the bachelor party."

"Oh Lord. Don't get in any trouble, dude. You've done so well."

"I'm only looking forward to the day I marry you, baby. Nothing else matters."

"Aww, that's so sweet. I'll let you get back to it."

"Thanks baby."

"Don't forget, you guys have to pick up the tux tomorrow."

"We haven't forgotten."

"Great. Good night, babe."

"Good night Karrington, my love."

She giggled at his comment. He would always say the sweetest things to her, and she loved him for it. It made all her problems go away. Karrington put on her headphones. She listened to her favorite gospel playlist. She needed that encouragement. After her shower, she went straight to bed to the gospel sounds.

The Doctor's Appointment

Karrington sat in the lobby of her doctor's office. She'd been there many times before. This felt different. She feared the worst. No matter what she did, her mind came back to that fear she would be the next Lewis woman to go down to the demonic cancer disease. When the nurse called her name, she jumped. The lady next to her rolled her eyes. Karrington wondered what she was thinking. She brushed it off and followed the nurse to the intake area.

The nurse said, "Good morning, Miss Lewis. How are you today?"

"Good morning. I'm okay, I guess. Just worried about these spots on my breast."

"I totally understand. Look, don't think about the worst. All you do is waste precious time worrying. Many times, these things are nothing to worry about. Dr. Chase will tell you more about it."

"Thanks. I appreciate your kind words." The nurse returned Karrington's smile and continued taking her vitals. Karrington wondered how she would tell Rich if the result was positive. She imagined he would take it hard. Nevertheless, she hoped he would stand by her no matter what. Both her father and grandfather died before their wives confronted their battles with cancer. She prayed that if she had it, Rich would stay by her side.

The nurse finished the vitals, "Dr. Chase will be with you in a minute."

"Thank you." Karrington stared at the walls of the tiny room. There were posters on the wall telling patients about different diseases and how to combat them. Karrington thought, *This is not the place to come if you are a hypochondriac.* She felt a drop of sweat on her back, followed by another and another. *Lord, please remove this anxiety from me.* She almost leapt out of her seat with the knock at the door. *I've got to stop that!* She announced, "Come in."

Dr. Chase walked through the door with a smile on her face. "Good morning, Miss Lewis. How are you today?"

"I'm… okay I guess."

"Yes, my nurse told me you were worried about a lump on your breast. Given your family history, that's understandable. However, you have to realize a lot of these are not cancerous." Karrington nodded her head. "So take your blouse off and let's have a look." Karrington complied. Dr. Chase examined her breast. "Is this one spot that concerns you?"

"Yes, ma'am."

"This one too?"

"Yes ma'am, and one here."

"Got you." Dr. Chase examined her closely. "Looks like you might have fibroadenoma. Have you heard of that?" Karrington shook her head. "Fibroadenoma is one of the most common types of non-cancerous breast tumors. It looks like a small marble that can be moved around under your skin. See how I do this?" Dr. Chase demonstrated what she was saying. Karrington started feeling better inside. "That rubbery feeling also tells me it's like a fibroadenoma. We will take some tests and get the results back."

"How fast will the results be back?"

"Hmm, we should know tomorrow around this time, but my best advice for you… don't worry, young lady. You'll outlive us all."

Karrington's smile lit up the room. "I just wanted to know before I got married Saturday."

"What? You should have led with that."

"Yes, I'm so excited."

"I bet you are! Congratulations. Not to worry, you go get married. Live a blessed life."

"Thank you, Dr. Chase."

"The nurse will come in and run some tests. We will get them to the lab and get your results as soon as possible. Once we know it is fibroadenoma we can set out a treatment for that."

"Sounds good Dr. Chase."

"Great, congratulations again."

Dr. Chase walked out of the office, and the nurse came in a few minutes later. Karrington couldn't wait to get out of the office and call Olivia. She knew she would be at her lunch with her mother's ex-boyfriend, so she would have to wait until after one to call. Once Karrington settled into her office, she handled one of her cases. She met with a client and had a sandwich while she made phone calls on her client's behalf. It was near two when she received a call from Olivia. "Hey, I was just about to call you, but I got sidetracked by this case."

"Hey Karrington. I understand. I've been waiting to hear what the doctor said."

"Dr. Chase is amazing. She put me at ease, then told me what she thought it was. She didn't think it was cancer. She ran the test to be sure. It looks like I'm in the clear."

"That's awesome Karrington. Now you can focus on your wedding."

Karrington noticed the sound of Olivia's voice. It wasn't that cheerful sound that she became accustomed to over the years. "Are you okay?" Olivia hesitated. "Olivia, come on, this is your bestie. What's wrong?" Karrington tried to sound happy in order to ease the sadness in her friend's heart.

"I lost a friend today."

"Oh no! Who, how?"

"We met when we first processed into the Air Force. We used to joke around a lot. Nothing relationship wise. We became really close friends. I went to Germany for three years for my first assignment. We kept in touch at least once a week. He was a fighter pilot. Today his plane went down. They said it was a mechanical issue." She cried. Karrington wanted to jump through the phone and be there for her friend. "I don't know what to do. I don't know his family or anything, but I need to reach out to them so I know when the funeral will be."

"Go ahead. What's stopping you?"

"Nothing. I'm just numb right now."

"I will finish what I'm doing and be right there for you."

"Thank you Karrington. I'm glad you're okay too."

"Thanks. I'll grab us some wine and we'll hang out tonight."

"I'll see you later, Karrington."

Karrington picked up a bottle of Chateau de Landiras 2018. The cashier said it was a great choice. Karrington wanted something to help her friend feel better. Although she realized nothing would really help her heal except time. She arrived at the building and went inside. Karrington knocked on the door. Olivia immediately opened. "Girl, were you standing by the door waiting for me?"

"No, I was actually waiting for the pizza to arrive. A sister starving."

"Oh good, I'm just in time then." Karrington took a seat on Olivia's chaise lounge. "Wine and pizza, a great combination."

"Yes, it is."

Olivia sat down with Karrington. Karrington didn't know what to say. Then the knock at the door came again. "I'll get it."

"No, I need to pay him."

"I can pay him."

"Karrington, I already have the cash set up. Sit down. I got this."

Karrington laughed, "Yes ma'am Captain ma'am." They both laughed. Karrington hoped to keep the laughter coming and take Olivia's mind off of her friend.

Olivia got the pizza. "You want a plate?"

"No, let's eat like we used to in high school, straight out of the box."

"Let's do it." Olivia grabbed the glasses for the wine, and they ate their pizza, listened to music, and talked. "Jeff and I were really close. I think if we were stationed together, we might have had a relationship. He was a good guy."

"Did you contact his family?"

"I did. They are making arrangements now. They will fly his body to Andrews Airforce Base on Monday. The funeral will be Saturday. How about that? I'll be glammed up for your wedding this Saturday and the following Saturday I'll be glammed up to say goodbye to my friend."

Karrington took her hand. "I can come back from my honeymoon early to go to the funeral with you."

"You better not! Your honeymoon is a once in a lifetime event. Enjoy it. I'm a big girl. I can handle it."

"You know I'll come back early, girl."

"I know you will, but you better not. That man's been waiting for some of that stuff all this time. Don't deprive him." Karrington burst out in laughter. Tears rolled down her eyes. Olivia touched her shoulder, "Look, that man has been waiting for you since high school. He would have a fit if you came back early."

"You are crazy, Olivia. Okay, I won't come back early, but I will be praying for you and his family."

"That's good enough, Karrington. Thank you." Olivia swallowed the last bite of her pizza. "So, what about you? Results come tomorrow. I hope you don't plan to ruin your wedding plans."

"I don't plan on it, no. But, if it's positive… Well, I don't know what to do at this point. I can't have him marry me and I won't be alive much longer."

Olivia choked on her wine. "Don't say that!" She stood up aggressively. "Karrington Lewis, don't ever say that again!"

Karrington realized she had struck a nerve with her friend. Before she could respond, she received a call from Betty, the wedding planner. "Hi Betty, I'm in the middle of something. What do you have for me?"

"Good evening, Miss Lewis. I believe we are all set for tomorrow at six. Everyone knows to be at the church for rehearsal. Have you heard from the maid of honor?"

"Yes, I'm with her now."

"Okay, she's the only one that hasn't checked in, will she be here tomorrow?"

"Yes, you can count on Olivia. She will be there. What about the dinner? Have all the arrangements been made for that?"

"Yes, Chef Daniels has everything arranged. It will be a delicious meal. I also have all the gifts ready for your bridal party."

"Thank you, Betty. You're wonderful."

"You're welcome. See you tomorrow evening."

"Good night." Karrington hung up the phone and refocused on Olivia. During Karrington's conversation with Betty, Olivia retook her seat. Karrington slid close to her and put her hand on her shoulder. She looked deeply into her eyes. For the first time, she could see the hurt and pain dwelling there. Karrington didn't know if it was because of her recent loss or the loss of her mother years ago, but the pain was there. Karrington softly said, "I'm sorry, my friend. I will never utter those words to you again. I promise."

The dam that held the pain back for Olivia burst. Tears gushed from her eyes. Karrington embraced her. She wanted to tell her it was okay, but she knew it wasn't. It wouldn't be for a while. The grief had to run its course before Olivia would be okay again. For now, she held her tight. If nothing else, Olivia knew Karrington was there for her.

The evening ended with Olivia falling asleep on the chaise lounge. Karrington eased out the door and locked it behind her. She had a key to Olivia's apartment for emergencies. Karrington drove home thinking about her friend and the deaths they both experienced in their lives. Karrington wanted this weekend to be about life and happiness. Somehow, death crept its way into the picture. *Lord, I know you are in control. Touch my friend Olivia and comfort her during this trying time. We both know the pain of loss, and we also know you. In your son Jesus' name… Amen.* After she closed out her prayer, Rich called. She was happy to hear his voice. "Hey babe. How are you?"

"I'm good. How is Olivia?"

"Struggling, but I know she'll be on point tomorrow. That military blood in her will get her through."

"Good. I can't wait until tomorrow's practice and of course, the main event. I have the tickets for our cruise, too."

"Awesome. Cancun will be a great way for us to start our long marriage."

"Amen baby. Well, I'm going to turn in for the night. I'll see you tomorrow."

"Good night, babe. I'm pulling up to the house."

"Great. I'll wait for you to get inside."

"Aww, you're so thoughtful. I'm out of the car and headed to the door. I know Aunt Lisa is probably sleeping in her favorite chair."

He laughed, "Probably. She's a great person, though."

"Yes, she is. I wish I had the chance to meet your family."

"Yeah, there's not many of them left. Those that are don't talk to me. I love your family. There are so many of them and you guys are strong and tight as a family. That's what I always wanted."

"We'll build our own."

"Let's do it!"

"Yes sir. I'm in the house. I was right, she is sleeping in that raggedy chair." She giggled. "Let me get her in bed. Good night, babe."

"Good night, sweetheart."

Karrington wrestled with Aunt Lisa. She eventually got her into her bed for the night. "Auntie, you need to lay off the wine." Karrington made it to the doorway.

"No, I don't." Aunt Lisa rolled over.

Karrington snickered, "I should have known you were awake." She went to her room and called it a night.

Karrington's Test Results

The morning sun smacked Karrington in the face. She used her hand to block it and rolled over, hoping to escape the sun's powerful rays. She moved away from its direct light, as the heat continued to pounce on her. *Darn it! I get to sleep in but can't. Lord, I guess you want me to get up.* Her feet hit the ground. She quickly hopped back into the bed. *I can't.* She laughed at herself. Her phone rang. It was Dr. Chase's office. *Oh my God.* "Hello."

A cheerful voice was on the other end. "Hello, may I speak to Karrington Lewis?"

"This is Karrington."

"Hi Miss Lewis, I have your lab results. I know you wanted to get them as soon as possible because you're getting married tomorrow. That's so awesome and I'm happy for you!"

"Why thank you. I appreciate that."

"Well, you have nothing to worry about. You don't have cancer. I believe Dr. Chase told you she believed you have fibroadenoma. Is that right?"

"Yes ma'am."

"So if you have a fibroadenoma that keeps growing or changing, Dr. Chase can operate to remove it. But this type of tumor usually stops growing or even shrinks without any treatment. Dr. Chase wants to monitor it for any changes. She wants you to come back in a month. She'll take another look at it, and we'll see where we're at. How's that sound?"

"That's wonderful, thank you."

"You're welcome. You can call us when you return from your honeymoon and schedule that appointment."

"I will do that. Again, thank you so much."

"You're welcome. Have a great day and an awesome wedding."

"Have a great weekend!" Karrington hung up the phone. She jumped out of bed with more excitement than she could have imagined. *I spent all that time worrying for nothing. Olivia was right. I should have trusted my Lord and Savior. Woo hoo! I'm healed. Better yet, I was never sick. Praise God!* Karrington hurried to get dressed. She had several errands to run before she met up with Olivia. Then they had more errands to run, including getting their hair done.

Karrington rushed around town getting items that she would need for her honeymoon. She wanted everything to be right. The news from Dr. Chase continually made her smile. She had a few minutes before meeting Olivia. A nice hot latte sounded good to her. Karrington pulled into a local bistro and grabbed a caramel macchiato. She enjoyed the feel of it rolling down her throat. Her eyes were closed. She wanted to enjoy every drop. When she opened her eyes, Olivia was giggling in front of her. "How long have you been standing there?"

"Only a few minutes, but it was worth it." Olivia sat down at the table. "Where's mine?"

"I left it at the counter for you. You didn't get it?" They both laughed. "Look, grab one and let's get going. We need to get to the hairdresser. You know how long they can take."

"Right, we need to be at the church at six."

They rushed to the hairdresser to get ready for the evening's events. Karrington forgot about her near cancer bout and Olivia appeared to put the death of her friend to the side. They both wanted to enjoy the weekend. Karrington asked Olivia, "I'm so nervous about tomorrow night, girl. I'm not afraid of the rehearsal, the wedding, the reception, any of that. What I'm most afraid of is when we get alone."

Olivia laughed, "The first time can be nerve wrenching, but you'll get through it."

"How was your first time?"

"Okay, we won't talk about my first time. It was nothing to talk about." Olivia frowned. "When I say nothing... I absolutely mean nothing!"

"Wow."

"Yeah, I was 15. Neither of us knew what we were doing. I should have waited until I was older and at least knew something. He didn't, and neither did I. The only good thing about it was we were both virgins. In hindsight, I should have lost it to someone who knew what they were doing."

"Well, I'm sure Rich knows what he's doing."

Olivia snapped her fingers. "Yep, that's for sure."

Karrington looked in the mirror. She loved her hairstyle. It was everything she wanted it to be. Olivia tapped the time on her phone, showing

Karrington they didn't have much time. Karrington said, "Okay, I'm coming." They rushed out the door, heading to the church. The rehearsal was the least of her worries, considering it all. She hoped the dinner would be great. Chef Daniels had a reputation for exceptional food and they were blessed to get him for the dinner and reception.

They were the last people to arrive at the church. Rich said, "My queen is here, everyone!" He hugged her tight. "I counted the minutes until your arrival."

"Oh, your comments keep turning me on."

"Baby, I will be by your side forever. I will never leave you or forsake you."

"Oh, now you're stealing God's word?" They laughed.

Pastor Henderson said, "Can we get started, please?"

Karrington and Rich giggled, pointing the finger at each other.

The rehearsal went as planned. The dinner was more than what Karrington could have expected. Everyone enjoyed it. Karrington felt honored by so many of her friends and family in the same room to celebrate her nuptials. The next day would be her best day ever. She kissed Rich at the car. He headed to his bachelor party while the girls headed to Olivia's apartment for their party.

The Wedding

Karrington waited in the back dressing room of the church. The day she waited for all her life was now upon her. Most women dream of this day. Karrington's dream included her parents and grandmother, but that wouldn't be possible. She was grateful that Aunt Liza became her surrogate mother. Her Uncle Benny stepped in to walk her down the aisle. She loved Uncle Benny. He was always the one all the cousins loved to see come through the door. He was direct, honest, and loving to all his nieces and nephews. She couldn't think of anyone else to do the honor of walking her down the aisle.

Karrington watched her bridesmaids and her maid of honor. They laughed and joked about everything. They were having the time of their lives while Karrington watched them with a smile. She spent most of her life making others happy. Now, on the biggest day of her life, she watched her friends laugh, and it filled her heart.

Olivia glanced at her, tilted her head to the side, then strolled over to Karrington. "What are you doing over here by yourself? This is your day."

"I know. I'm just taking it all in right now. Watching all of you enjoy this time is enjoyable for me."

Olivia rolled her head back, "If you don't get up and have some fun." Olivia pulled her by the arm.

"The photographer is coming in to get some shots and video. People need to see you happy. Not sitting there taking it all in." The other ladies chimed in, encouraging Karrington to get up and join the fun. As she did she pushed the emotions of health and grief behind her. Today was her day. Nothing would stop the fun.

The time came when Karrington was about to walk down the aisle. *This is every woman's dream*, she thought as she suppresses the nervousness running rampant through her body. *Lord, I can't fall down. Don't let me make a fool of myself!* She giggled at the thought of falling. It would make a great memory to tell her children. It would also be embarrassing now. She tried not to look at the people in the pews. Everyone was focused on her.

The whisper from the kind loving man whose arm she held brought comfort to her spirt, *"Don't worry, sweetheart. You got this. Enjoy your moment."*

She looked at him with a smile. She loved her uncle. He always knew what to say and when to say it. The closer she got to Rich, the faster her heartbeat sped up. The time came when she would release her uncle's arm and take the man's arm who would be her husband. She stared through the veil at him with a love she never believed she would display for a man. He charmed her heart. She was ready to say the magical words, 'I do.'

After the wedding, Karrington's nerves returned to normal. The excitement of the photo session soothed her soul. She was now united with the man she loved. Olivia whispered in her ear, "Are you ready to give it up?"

Karrington pushed her lovingly, "You know it."

The two longtime friends laughed like they were sisters. Jalen walked up to his sister, "Hey sis, I got to say I'm happy for you. I hope everything goes well. Rich was a jerk in high school. He seems to have changed... a lot!"

"Thank you, baby brother. I'm glad you could get some time off to come see your sister get married."

"Of course. I told them they had to let me go. Although, I do have to leave early in the morning. We have a two o'clock game tomorrow."

"I totally understand. Go score a touchdown."

Jalen laughed. "You're joking, right?"

"Yes baby bro, I'm joking. I know you score baskets."

"Stop it Karrington. Homeruns baby, that's what I'm about."

Karrington punched him lightly. "I know. Seriously though, I hope you hit more home runs than anyone else in the league. Get to the majors, man!"

"I will."

Jalen kissed her on the cheek and made his way to the reception area. Karrington returned to her photoshoot with her new husband. Rich said, "Jalen seems happy with us."

"He is. I'm happy too, you know."

"I certainly hope so, Mrs. Johnson."

"Oh, the first time! I'm going to melt."

"You can't melt yet, baby."

"Are you getting fresh, Mr. Johnson?"

"Yeah."

They both laughed. After the photoshoot the Johnsons went into the reception area. Karrington was knocked off her feet when Rich gave a speech. "Everyone, I just want to say a few words. First, thank you all for coming out to see Karrington and myself unite as one. I met Karrington in high school and trust me, we never thought we would be in this position." He paused, looked down, and then back up again. "I knew Karrington was special, but I was trapped being the jerk that I was. I thought I was all that, as they say. Every college in the country wanted me to play football for them. People, especially girls, idolized me. I could have anyone I wanted. However, the one I wanted didn't want me." He stroked

Karrington's chin. She smiled up at him. "When I suffered my career ending injury, I discovered how a man could be on top of the world one day, then on the bottom of the world the next day. All those people who called me their friend suddenly couldn't be found. I was alone, my wife divorced me and married my replacement. I thought about killing myself." Everyone gasped.

Karrington took his hand. She wanted to tell him he didn't need to do this, but he stroked her chin again, telling her nonverbally that it was okay.

He continued. "Then one day I remembered what that girl used to say. The one who didn't want me. She always told me to get my education. Someday football wouldn't work for me, but my education would. I refocused my energy. A few years later, I got my degree, which led me to a great job. I always wanted to thank that girl who grew up to be an amazing woman. I was blessed with the opportunity in front of a coffee shop four months ago. Now, I'm the luckiest man in the world because that woman is now my wife." The applause was deafening. Karrington nearly cried, as she fought back the tears.

"Karrington, I want to say that I love you and I will never leave your side. No matter what we face in this life, we will face it together as husband and wife!"

Karrington stood up. She hugged him tightly. The couple kissed deeply. Everyone wooed at the couple. Olivia shouted, "Let's have some dance music!"

Karrington said, "You can count on Olivia to get the party started."

"May I have the first dance?"

"Yes you may, honey!"

The reception went well into the night before the happy couple returned to their limousine. Everyone waved at them as they pulled off, headed to their hotel for the night. Tonight would be their first romantic night together, and Karrington's stomach could attest to her nervousness. She tried her best to hold it in, not wanting Rich to know how nervous she really was. She wanted to please him, except she had no experience.

They arrived at the hotel and everyone they met paused for the couple. Karrington felt like a *Hollywood* star. So many people told her how beautiful she looked. This would truly be a day she would remember forever.

Once in the room, Karrington pulled out her night clothes and made a beeline to the bathroom. She thought she would throw up. *Come on girl, you got this. Your new husband is waiting for you.* She pulled herself together and got dressed. She laughed to herself, *This is crazy. I'm dressing just to get undressed. I hope he likes this nightgown. It was the sexiest one they had.* Once she finished, she looked in the mirror for one last gaze. Here goes nothing. She turned the doorknob and walked out. The room was partially lit. Rich had nightlights plugged in around the room. Her foot felt something between her toes. She looked down and gasped. She laughed with happiness, "You put rose petals on the floor. How sweet."

"I wanted my queen to walk on them for her first time."

"Aww." She made her way to the bed, where Rich waited. There were two glasses of wine waiting on the bedside table. Rich handed her one, and he took the other. "You thought of everything, Mr. Johnson."

"Just for you Mrs. Johnson." She started to drink, but he stopped her. "Hold on there, missy." They both chuckled, "This is a toast to everlasting love. May today be our beginning, and we never see an end."

"Amen!"

The couple drank their wine. The evening began. Karrington's nervousness turned to excitement and joy. She loved every moment of it. In her heart, this was the beginning of a never-ending love.

5 – Six Months Later

After six months of marriage, there wasn't anything in her life that wasn't going well for Karrington. Rich got a promotion at his job. They were set financially, and Olivia found someone to love.

Karrington was in the middle of the biggest case of her brief career. She was defending a man accused of murdering his wife. Tyre Swift was a millionaire basketball player who many believed was sleeping around on his wife. For that alone, Karrington despised him. She had to represent him anyway. They found Tyre with the murder weapon in his apartment, and his fingerprints were not on it. Karrington believed she could get him off because others who were in the apartment had access to the gun.

Karrington waited at her favorite bistro for Olivia. Their rendezvous became a bi-weekly event for them to catch up with the goings on of their lives. Olivia was late. She pulled up her chair. Karrington slid a hot coffee over to her with a smile that stated the obvious, "You late, O."

"I know, I know. I had to get away from the colonel then Maurice called me whining about not seeing me much. Ugh, if I didn't love him, I'd kick him to the curb."

Karrington burst out in laughter. "You two are something else. When is he going to pop the question?"

"Don't ask me, ask him… tonight, at dinner."

"I will not put that man on the spot like that."

Olivia took a sip of her coffee. "Look, my time here is counting down. I'm due for an assignment at any time. The brother needs to get his act together or I'm out of here. When the Air Force says go, I have to go. You know what I mean?"

"I know exactly what you mean. I'll ask tonight." Karrington stared off into the afternoon sky. She loved spending time with Olivia, but today she was distracted by other things. She asked, "How's your family?"

"Everyone is good. Yours?"

"Not so good. Aunt Lisa is struggling. You know she's too proud to ask for help. I have to do things on the down low, so she doesn't know."

"She's always been someone who could take care of herself. I can understand."

"I can too, but she was always there for me, so let me return the favor."

"Karrington, they don't always see it like that. My uncle was the same way before he passed. Dude was 84 years old and determined to take care of himself right until the end. Stubborn old man. We just

76

brought groceries over and put them in the house, paid his bills and whatever else he needed. He grumbled, oh well, but we needed to do what we needed to do."

"That's what I'm going to do then." She gave a high five to Olivia. "In fact, before dinner, I think I'm going to show up there with some things I know she likes. She'll say some stuff, but she'll get over it too."

"How's that case going?"

"Okay for now. I really hate defending this cheater."

"Duty calls sister."

"Yes, it does. He's so arrogant too. Did you know he hit on me?"

"What?"

"He sure did! His wife hasn't been gone long, and he's trying to get a date with another married woman, me. The nerve of him. He thinks the world owes him something."

"That's how some of these guys from the hood are. They make it to the big time and think everyone is supposed to bow to them. I wouldn't date any of them."

"Me either." Karrington got up. "I have to get back and prepare this brief for this man's court date next week. I can't wait to see you guys tonight. It's going to be fun."

"Yes, it is." Olivia stood. They hugged. "I'm going to enjoy the rest of my coffee. I'll see you tonight."

"Yes, ma'am." Karrington hurried across the street to her car. She drove back to work listening to music. She ordered groceries for Aunt Lisa when she arrived at the office. *I pray she doesn't send the poor people away when they arrive with her groceries.* Her desk phone rang. "This is Karrington Lewis. May I help you?"

"Yes, Miss Lewis, this is Angie from Dr. Chase's office. We noticed you didn't make your appointment. Do you wish to reschedule?"

Darn it, I completely forgot. "I'm sorry, I've been bogged down on this court case and forgot. When can I reschedule?"

"Can you come in Tuesday at 10?"

"Yes, I will mark it on my calendar and be there. Thank you so much."

"You're welcome."

Karrington hung up the phone. She stared at the computer. Going to the doctor was not something she enjoyed doing anymore. The pain of waiting for results was not something she looked forward to. Watching her mother and grandmother endure it was no fun. Now her aunt was suffering too.

78

I guess that's the price I pay for being one of the youngest grandkids in the family. I get to watch all of my aunts and uncles leave this world. Let me get some work done before this day is over.

Karrington buried herself in her work, making the time fly by. She got the call from her aunt, scolding her while thanking her for the groceries. Karrington simply laughed, knowing she did the right thing. Her aunt's condition came on fast. Karrington would never give up hope that Aunt Lisa would stay a little longer just for her.

Karrington rose out of her seat. The restaurant was calling her name. She raced by the house first to shower and change. Hopefully Rich would be there already. If he were dressed, they could head out quickly. *This sister is starving. I can't wait to get my mouth on that ribeye. It's so delicious.*

She arrived at the house, and Rich's car was in the garage. *Yes! Now please be dressed, dude.* She walked into the house and Rich sat on the couch sipping on a drink. *I have such a wonderful life!* "Hi honey, I'm so glad you're here… and you're dressed. I love it."

"Yeah, I got off a little early and came straight home."

She noticed the look of concern on his face. It was a look that Karrington realized she would not like. She asked, "Is everything okay?"

"Yeah, everything is cool… sort of."

"Sort of Rich? It either is or it's not. Let's not start having secrets, dude."

He sighed, dropped his head, then slowly raised it up. "It's Diedre. She called me today, asking how I was doing. She wanted to meet up with me tonight. Of course I told her no."

Karrington didn't know what to feel inside. She didn't trust this man in high school. However, after reuniting with him six months ago, they married and were happy. At least she thought they were happy. "What does she want to meet about?"

"I don't know, and I don't care. That life is behind me. I'm telling you because you know Diedre, and when she wants something, she goes for it."

"But you don't know what she wants."

"No, I don't." He paused. "I also don't care what she wants. What I want is right here with me. I love you baby and through thick and thin, I will be here with you."

"Okay. Well, I'm going to get dressed. A sister is hungry." She forced a smile on her face, but she wasn't happy to hear Diedre resurfaced in their life. She kissed him on the lips and hurried to get a shower and change.

In the shower, she heard Rich shouting. She froze and allowed the water to cover her body. She clutched her hands together, letting her chin rest on them. The tears were attempting to force their way out of her eyes. Karrington was known as a crier, and it didn't take much for the tears to roll down her face. At least while the water was hitting her face, no one could tell she was crying. *I can't believe this is happening. Something is going on and he's not telling me the whole story. We've been married for six months, and this woman is coming back into his life. How does she have his cell number? We purchased new cell numbers together. There is no reason she should have that number! I am going to get to the bottom of this for real!* Karrington stepped out of the shower and dried herself off. She walked into the bedroom covered in only her towel. Rich sat on the bed. Karrington froze, waiting for what she was sure would be bad news.

"She insists I meet her tonight."

"You're not going." She moved to her closet to retrieve her dress. "If you go, Rich, don't come back."

"Honey—"

"Honey nothing! You have no reason to go see her… none! You're my husband. This isn't high school Rich. It's me or her."

"Then I won't go see her."

"Never Rich!"

"Never."

Rich stood and walked out of the room. She didn't know if she could trust him. She looked in the mirror while holding her favorite flowered dress up to her body. The evening that she looked forward to so much was turning bad. *Chef Daniels, you better make that ribeye extra special tonight. I need some food in me before I hurt someone.*

After she finished dressing, Karrington came out to the living room. Rich was watching sports news. He stood up, "Are you ready?"

"Yes, honey."

"Hey look, I'm sorry about all of this, but let's not let it ruin our evening."

"Too late." She walked toward the door, stopping short of it. She turned and looked at him to open the door. He did. She walked through to the passenger side of the car and repeated the same. He opened her door, and she sat inside. Typically, she didn't insist on these acts of a gentleman. Tonight, was different. She wore her anger well and wanted him to embrace it fully. Karrington dealt with Diedre in high school. She was not dealing with her now.

They arrived at Chef Daniels' restaurant. Olivia and Maurice had arrived and been seated. Olivia motioned for them to join them. Karrington hugged her best friend, "You're awfully excited tonight. Anything I should know?"

Olivia poked Karrington in the shoulder, "No… don't start."

"Okay, I won't. Guess who reared her ugly head again?"

Rich said, "Honey…" Karrington rolled her eyes at him. "Look, let's order a bottle of wine and enjoy the evening."

Olivia smacked her lips, "Um, I want to know who reared her ugly head. Forget the wine… for now."

Maurice chimed in, "Honey, it's clear Rich doesn't want to talk about it."

Karrington kept silent. Part of her wished she hadn't said anything, but another part of her wanted to bring it all out. She looked at Rich, "My apologies. Let's do as my husband wishes. We shouldn't be talking about that now."

"Well dang," shrugged Olivia. "Can you give a sister a hint?" Karrington rolled her eyes in that now famous stop asking look. "Okay, wine it is."

The evening progressed better than it started. Karrington pushed Diedre into the back of her mind. She enjoyed the banter between the couples. She believed Maurice was a good man for Olivia. "So, what's the future looking like for the two of you?"

Rich laughed, "Karrington?"

"What? I need to know if I should look at dresses or not."

Maurice said, "It's a fair question." He paused and turned toward Olivia. Karrington's excitement rose. She could only imagine the same for Olivia. Karrington positioned herself, poised to hear the question she hoped would come.

Maurice took Olivia's hand. "I was going to do this later, when we were alone. Karrington seems to have jumped into my mind." Olivia braced herself. Karrington could read her like a book. Olivia was excited and scared. Karrington matched her excitement and fear. She kicked herself for being scared. This was a moment a woman remembered forever. Fear wasn't something to be associated with it, but she was scared nonetheless. Maurice continued, "In life a man searches for his mate, but truly we only find one. It then becomes a matter of realizing who that one is and making her yours forever. I realized it almost immediately when I met you that you were my 13th rose." Olivia's brow rose. "What I mean is a dozen roses is a way of saying I love you but when that dozen surrounds a single white rose, that means you've found the one that stands out. The one that you will love forever." Olivia smiled and glanced at Karrington.

Karrington's fists were clinched, waiting for the question so she could explode. Maurice reached into his pocket and pulled out the box. He opened it, then asked, "Olivia, will you marry me?"

Olivia placed her hand over her mouth. Karrington jumped up and down in her seat. She wanted to scream but contained herself waiting for Olivia's answer. Olivia simply said, "Yes."

Karrington jumped up and grabbed her friend. They both jumped up and down while hugging each other, screaming sounds of happiness. Karrington let go, then hugged Maurice. "You've got yourself a winner. Congratulations." Everyone in the restaurant clapped with happiness. Olivia was the center of attention. Karrington knew the feeling from her wedding day. Now it was her turn to be the maid of honor. "I can't wait to see you walk down that aisle, Olivia!"

"I can't wait to walk it too!"

They ended on a happy note. Each couple went their own way. On the ride home, Karrington wanted to address the Diedre issue. It was late and she decided to forget about it. She reasoned Rich didn't want to talk about it either. They both remained quiet on the ride. They pulled into the garage. Karrington got out of the car. She noticed Rich huff because she didn't wait for him to open her door. She blew him a kiss, not because she loved him, she did. She blew him a kiss because she wanted to antagonize him.

They reached the bedroom still without speaking to each other. Karrington went into the bathroom and dressed for bed. When she came out, she noticed Rich was prepared for sex. In those moments when he wanted to have sex, he wouldn't wear anything to bed. *He's going to get his feelings hurt tonight.* Karrington made sure she wore her complete pajama set, leaving no room for Rich to think sex would happen.

He said, "I guess nothing is going to happen tonight."

She laughed, then rolled over. He grumbled and rolled the other way. He didn't respond, the way she wanted him to respond and that made her angrier. Finally, she abruptly turned over, "So you're not even going to say anything about Diedre?" He sighed. "You seriously think you're going to get something from me when you're still talking to Diedre? Get real." She abruptly turned her back to him. After a while, she drifted off to sleep. An hour later, she woke up. Rich wasn't in bed. Karrington got up. She leaned her ear into the air, thinking she heard talking. It sounded like a mumble coming from the bathroom. She got up, but Rich came out of the bathroom. "You've got to be kidding me? You're in the bathroom talking to that woman?"

"I was talking to Jermaine."

"Right." Karrington threw Rich's pillow at him. "Sleep on the couch." Rich grumbled something and walked into the living room. "Say it louder." He didn't respond. *This is not going to be a good weekend.* Karrington laid back down and fell asleep.

Saturday morning brought with it a raging storm outside Karrington's window. The wind and rain woke her from her sleep. She looked over and Rich was in the bed. *I thought I told him the couch was for him last night.* She got up and went to the bathroom to wash up. When she finished, she heard Rich moving around the bedroom. She walked out but refused to say anything to him. Karrington didn't want to fight. She knew something was going on with Diedre, and she would not let this day go by without finding out. Her phone buzzed, and she picked it up. Olivia sent a text to her. It read, *"Karrington, did you see the news about Micah Hill? He was cut by Denver. They say he was using performance enhancing drugs. Diedre's world is over. That's probably why she was reaching out to your man. She wants him back because he's making all that bank right now."* Karrington frowned. *So that's it and he's not telling me because this fool wants to go back to her.* Rich sat on the bed, looking at his phone. She said, "So there you have it. Micah gets cut by Denver and now she wants you back." She paused. "I don't know what's worse; her bouncing from man to man or you running back to her whenever she calls."

Rich stood up and faced Karrington. "I'm not running anywhere. I told her I couldn't meet with her last night or any night. If she had something to say to me, she needed to say it over the phone or through text." He paused and looked down as if his phone were going to do the talking for him. "She called last night. That's when you got really mad. She wanted to tell me I'm the father of her son." The look on Karrington's face could crush a diamond. "I know what you're thinking. She told me it was Micah's baby, and I went with it. Now she's changing her story since he got cut. Unlike me, he has no education to fall back on."

Karrington stood in disbelief. She couldn't believe she was back in high school again. She got the man, but here comes his ex-again. "I… I don't know what to say, Rich. I married you thinking this high school stuff was over. It's far from over. She's still playing her games, and it still involves you. How does she have your phone number? Before you answer, you know I got these cells after we got married. She shouldn't have this number." She tilted her head, waiting for an answer.

"She called my office asking to speak with me. I told her I had to go to a meeting. That's when I gave her my number and told her to call me later."

"You shouldn't have done that. She's after your money. Get a paternity test as soon as possible and if it's your child… well, I don't know what to say if it's your child."

"If it's my child, it's from a time before you. The child is 18 months old Karrington."

"I know it's before me, but if it's yours, you will be involved with her for the rest of your life. That's not what I signed up for. Frankly, I don't know if I would have signed up for this if I knew that six months ago." It was tough for her to speak through her tears. She was tired of the Rich, Diedre dynamic. She wanted it to be over, but somehow, she returned to his life. This time, it had to end.

"I'm going to a clinic this morning. It's one she has nothing to do with. They will take my sample and test it against the child. The clinic will get the sample from the doctor she takes her son to. That way, we know it's all legitimate, and no one can tamper with it."

"Good. I'll go with you." She walked over and placed her hands on his shoulders. "What do you want the result to be?"

"I want it to be negative. I want my children from one mother… you."

The comment may not be true, but she enjoyed hearing him say it anyway. She loved him and this isn't his fault, but it was another obstacle to go through in their marriage.

After Rich provided his DNA sample, the couple went to a local spot for breakfast. Karrington wanted to enjoy the day together. She thought about reaching out to Olivia to start planning the wedding, but that could wait. The night before wreaked havoc on their marriage. It was time for some repair work.

The rest of the weekend went by well. Karrington and Rich came to an agreement about Diedre and the baby. Karrington talked to Aunt Lisa about Rich's pending paternity. There was nothing she could do if the baby turned out to be Rich's child. Karrington hoped this was another scam by Diedre and it would blow over before she knew it.

It was Tuesday morning, and Karrington had to go to her doctor's appointment. It was routine enough for her. Nothing exciting. Taking tests always embodied fear for her because of her family history. She was happy Aunt Lisa was doing better. The doctors were upbeat about her treatment. She was in her 60s and Karrington always worried about her. Many family members didn't live to see their 60s, Aunt Lisa was the exception. She reminded herself that after these tests, she wouldn't have to do it again for a year. Each successful test result was like a new lease on life for Karrington.

After her doctor's visit, Karrington worked on her case. The next day would be spent giving opening statements at court. She spent hours working on her brief and statement. It needed to be perfect. The phone rang. "Hey Olivia, what's up?"

"Nothing, just counting these hours down. Me and Maurice are going to the movies tonight. You guys should come too."

"I can't O. I got this case kicking off tomorrow. I need to be ready, girl."

"That monster. Let them send him to jail for life."

"Come on O, everyone deserves a good defense. Innocent until proven guilty."

"You think he did it?"

"I can't afford to think one way or the other. He's my client and my job is to get the best result for him. That's what I'm going to do."

"You're saying all the right buzzwords. Good for you. When I get in trouble, I know who to call."

"You better not get your little butt in trouble."

"No girl, you know I can't do that. I got a husband now."

"Y'all ain't married yet."

"Look at you, sounding all down south." They laughed. Karrington and Olivia always had a good time together. "Anyway, let me go make my rounds. I need to make sure them cops on the ball."

"How is it again you became head of the Security Police?"

"That dang criminal justice degree. My sister talked me into it. Said it would open doors for me. She loves being in a legal office. I hate working this shift work."

"Cross train."

"I want to, but we'll see. Anyway, I got to go."

"Okay, take care."

"You too, Karrington."

Karrington hung up and returned to her work. Before she knew it, the clock read seven. She was curious why Rich hadn't called, so she called him. The phone went to voicemail. Karrington finished her work and headed home. It was nine. *I hope he cooked something. I'm starving.* The ride home was quiet. She didn't feel like music pounding her ears. Instead, she listened to the road under her car as she drove. Once home, she realized Rich wasn't there. Thoughts of him and Diedre rushed into her mind. She fought them off, not wanting to imagine him returning to his roots. When he walked in, Karrington was sitting at the breakfast bar.

"Where have you been, baby?" Rich asked.

"Where have I been? I called you and your phone went straight to voicemail. Where's your car?"

"Okay, I lost my phone. It must be in the car. I had an accident, and they towed my car. It might be totaled. I'll hear from the insurance agent tomorrow. My phone is probably in the car."

"Are you okay?"

"Yeah, I'm good. I can't say the same about my car, though."

"Well, I can give you a ride to work in the morning. What's for dinner?"

"I ordered out. Thai food. I can warm it up for you."

"That would be awesome. I'm going to get changed. Pour me some wine too, please."

"You got it, baby."

She walked into the bedroom. Karrington sat on the bed for a minute, relishing in her thoughts. *It was good I didn't continue that thought of him being with Diedre. There was a reasonable thought behind everything. Back off enemy!* Karrington quickly got dressed and returned to the breakfast bar. Rich had her food piping hot for her. "Thank you, honey. I am so hungry right now."

"I bet you are. How's the case coming?"

"Good. Tomorrow is the opening statement. It's going to be a long day for me."

"Well, I will try to have something good for you to eat when you get home."

"That would be awesome."

"By the way, I also have an update on Diedre and the baby."

"Can I eat first? I don't want to eat and be angry."

"You won't be."

Karrington replied. "Okay, great!"

"She never took the child to give his DNA. What does that tell you?"

"She was lying just to get you back. She didn't think you would call her bluff."

"Exactly. I expected as much, though. Diedre is cunning, but I wasn't born yesterday."

Karrington snickered, "The day before maybe."

He put his hand on her shoulder. "You got jokes."

The rest of the evening went great for Karrington and Rich. She enjoyed the wine by the fireplace with her husband. The days of Diedre were over, and she could enjoy life with Rich.

The morning came quicker than Karrington expected. She dressed in her best business suit, prepared for court. Karrington dropped Rich off at a rental car agency and headed to work. She needed to finalize everything before she headed to court. She said to her secretary, "Hey, make sure they have my client ready for me to meet with prior to court."

"Yes ma'am."

Karrington smiled. She told her secretary several times not to call her ma'am. Mattie, her secretary, was older than her, but she was raised to call all people sir or ma'am who were over her. Karrington respected that, so she stopped asking her not to say it. Karrington got her things together, sipped on her coffee, then headed to court.

Karrington spoke to her client, then sat at the defense table, waiting for the judge to arrive. She worked on a couple of cases since she passed the bar, but this judge was new to her. Karrington heard he was tough, and hoped he would be fair, especially with a new attorney. She glanced over at her client. He had no cares in the world. Tyre expected to be vindicated, even though Karrington's gut told her he was guilty. She couldn't let that stop her from defending him. Karrington's phone vibrated. It was her doctor's office calling. The nerves of starting her biggest case were fully implanted. A call from her doctor increased the intensity. She felt herself perspiring and tried to stop it. Aunt Lisa told her once that when anxiety reared its head that she should think about calming things. Karrington focused on a beach she once visited, hoping the anxiety would go away. The judge walked out. The bailiff summoned everyone to rise. Court was about to begin.

The judge conducted the preliminary actions. Karrington tried hard to focus. Her mind continued to wonder what her doctor wanted. She brushed it off. It was time for opening statements. Her peer with the district attorney's office, Becky White, went to the same law school as she did. They were a year apart, so Becky had more experience than Karrington.

Becky started her opening statement from her seat. "Ladies and gentlemen of the court. We're here today for you to determine the guilt or innocence of Tyre Swift." She stood and moved toward the jury. "Now the defense would have you believe that Tyre Swift had nothing to do with the murder of his wife. That isn't true at all. They would have you believe he was not in town when the murder occurred. We concede that issue, but our case is based on the contract between Tyre Swift and Blaine Dickerson. Tyre contacted Blaine via the dark web to have his wife murdered. We will prove this by witness testimony, message transcripts and testimony from Blaine himself. It is up to you to draw the correct conclusion that Tyre Swift made a contract with Blaine Dickerson to have his wife murdered. The prosecution believes that you will come to that conclusion. Thank you for your time."

Becky took her seat. Karrington paused for a moment. She looked at her phone, but changed her mind. She didn't want her mind cluttered with whatever they wanted to tell her.

Karrington rose and stood squarely in front of the jury. She pursed her lips and started, "Ladies and gentlemen of the jury, this case isn't as simple as my colleague wants you to believe. We have one man's word that a contract was made. He says this only after the district attorney arrested him on unrelated charges and offered him a deal for less time in jail. Wouldn't you say anything to get that? I'm sure anyone would."

She paused, "My client is an athlete and many of his haters, for lack of a better word, would love to see him go down. He's brash, arrogant, and maybe he puts off people a bit because he's good at his profession. However, that doesn't mean he killed the woman he loved so dearly. We will show that the couple had plans. Why would a man plotting to kill his wife have plans to take her to Cancun? It's simple. He had nothing to do with this crime. All we are asking you is to look at the evidence and make a good conscience decision based on the facts. We believe if you do that, you will determine his innocence. Thank you."

Karrington returned to her seat as the proceedings continued with the prosecution's case. The morning session rolled by. Karrington felt good about her case and the direction it was headed. The judge released them for lunch. She wanted to call the doctor, but she needed to gather some information in response to two of the prosecution's witnesses. She believed she could contradict them in her cross examination. Karrington rushed back to her office, making phone calls on the way. The 45-minute break wasn't nearly enough to get the items she needed. But she had to try.

Before she knew it, Karrington found herself back at the defense table. She had nothing to eat and barely got her evidence together. What she didn't get to do was call Dr. Chase's office. Right before she picked up her phone to dial the number, the judge returned to the courtroom. The afternoon proceedings continued until late. Karrington briefed her client on the day's events, then the guards escorted him back to his holding cell. She sat for a moment to take a breath. Becky asked her, "You're that tired, old lady."

Karrington chuckled, "I am. I don't know why, but not to worry; you won't get the win on this one." They chuckled. "How about I buy you a drink?"

"I want to, but I can't. I actually have a hot date tonight. First one in months."

"Oh, good for you." She patted Becky on the shoulder. "I guess I'll head home to my husband."

"Take care Karrington."

"You too, Becky." Karrington headed to her car. She wanted to get home, eat and get some much needed rest. She didn't understand why she felt so tired. She believed a little rest would cure that. Karrington parked in the usual spot in the garage. She wondered, *Hmm, why isn't he home yet?* Her question was answered when the lights hit her. Rich was pulling in right behind her. She stopped and waited for him to park. Once Rich reached the door, she hugged and kissed him. "Your wife is tired, baby. It was a long day in court."

"I imagined it would be." He kissed her again. "I had a long day too, so let's order out."

"You got it. What are we going for, Indian… Italian, what?"

"How about a good ole American cheeseburger and fries?"

Karrington burst out in laughter. "Really? You know I can go for that too. I would love a Coke with it."

"Awesome. I placed the order. They should be here in thirty. In the meantime, let's both freshen up."

"Why, Rich, are you trying to seduce me?"

"I would, but that might take longer than 30 minutes, honey."

"We can have a quicky."

"What? You're suggesting that?"

"Okay, I'm a little on the wild side today. I told you I'm tired, and it's been a long day. Get it in while you can because after I eat, I'm going to cuddle up in the bed and see where my sleep takes me."

"Then how can I pass up an offer like that? It's on."

The couple headed to the bedroom to make love while they waited for their food to arrive. After dinner, Karrington kept her word and cuddled up in the bed to watch her favorite shows. It wasn't long before those shows were watching her.

Karrington woke up in the middle of the night. Rich hadn't come to bed. She walked out to the living room. "Honey, I'm still tired. I don't know why I'm so tired lately." She looked around and Rich was nowhere to be seen. She looked in the garage. His rental car was gone. *Hmm, he must have gone out with the boys. No more accusations from this girl. I'm headed back to bed.* Karrington returned to the bed and fell asleep again. This time, she woke up with the alarm.

Rich woke up with her. He said, "Hey, you must have been sound asleep last night."

"I was for a while. When I woke up, you were gone."

"One of my coworkers was buying drinks at Timothy's. I went down there and had a couple with them. You were out, and it was real early."

"I drifted off early. I don't know why I'm so tired. I need to get dressed and head in for court. The judge don't play." She giggled as she went into the bathroom to get dressed for the day.

On her ride to the courthouse, Karrington stopped and grabbed a cup of coffee. While in line, she got a text from the clerk letting her know court would start at nine instead of eight. *Outstanding, an hour to enjoy my coffee and a Danish. Praise God.* She remembered that she now had time to follow up with her doctor. Before she could call, Dr. Chase's office called her. She felt that pit in her stomach each time her doctor's office called, wondering if this was the moment she would be told she's next.

She answered the phone carefully. "Hello."

"Hi Miss Lewis, this is Angie from Dr. Chase's office. How are you today?"

"Depends on what you're going to tell me." Karrington expected her to laugh, but she didn't. *That's not a good sign.* "I'm doing well. I just have a big court case going on today."

"Oh, the Tyre case? I saw you on the news. Good luck."

"Thank you."

"Dr. Chase would like to have you retake your blood test. She sent over the slips to the lab. All you have to do is go and let them draw blood. Make sure you fast eight hours beforehand."

"Thank you. What is her concern?"

"Uh, I'm not sure. All she asked me to do was to ask you to go back to the lab. I can leave a message for her to contact you. I know you're busy with the case and all, but she can probably call you in the evening. Would that work?"

"Yes, that would be fine. Thank you."

"You're welcome."

"I will go over to the lab as soon as I can. There's one about a block from here. I'll see if I can get in there."

"That's great Miss Lewis. Good luck again with the case."

"Thank you Angie. Have a great day."

"You, too!"

Karrington hung up the phone. She tried not to think about the reasoning behind the retest. She needed to focus on her defense for her client. *Whatever happens will happen. I can't sit here and worry about it. Lord, you are in control. I give it all to you.* The judge joined them in the courtroom. The case started for the day, keeping Karrington's mind focused on the law instead of her medical issues.

The judge released everyone for lunch. Karrington used the time to head down to the lab. She knew one of the techs and hoped she could get her in during lunch. Before she arrived at the lab, she called Penny Davis. "Hey Penny, this is Karrington."

"Karrington... the big time lawyer we all see on television."

"Hey girl, I'm sorry I haven't had a chance to reach out."

"Don't apologize. You got a lot going on, so I understand. What you need?"

"I have more lab tests to run and I'm only at lunch for 45 minutes. This judge is a stickler for punctuality."

"I got you. Come in and tell the person at the counter you have an appointment with me."

"Will do. Thank you, Penny. I owe you."

"Alright, that ribeye from Chef Daniels."

"You got it, girl. See you in a few."

"Okay, see you."

Karrington hung up. She was in front of the lab. She went inside and told the person at the counter she had an appointment with Penny. It didn't take long to get her test completed. She wanted to ask Penny what the test was about, but she decided not to involve her in her medical history any more than she needed to be. The two ladies hugged, and Karrington returned to court for the afternoon session.

The afternoon went well. The prosecution continued their case while Karrington continued to poke holes in it. She felt she was doing well. Her manager spent the day in court watching her. He confirmed Karrington's belief. That brought a good feeling to her. At the end of the day, she felt tired again. The feeling of fatigue worried her because that's how her mother felt before they diagnosed her. Hopefully, Dr. Chase would call her that evening and tell her something. She called Olivia on her ride home. "Hey O, how are you?"

"I'm good. A long day planning the wedding. We decided on next month in Cancun."

"What?"

"Yeah, we want to do a little something different from everyone else. We believe all our friends can afford a trip to Mexico, so hopefully…"

"Count me in, girl. I will be there."

"You need to be there. You're my maid of honor. There's no wedding without you."

"I know that's right. Thanks for lifting my spirits."

"The case isn't going well?"

"Actually, I might get this guy off. I'm also believing he's innocent myself."

"Really? Well, good for you. What's got you down?"

"Same as usual."

"Come on Karrington? You can't go through life thinking every little thing is cancer." There was silence. Karrington didn't know how to respond. "Karrington, you don't have cancer. Stop listening to that demon."

"I tried, but things just keep being there. I need help. I know it."

"Why are you thinking about it now?"

"Dr. Chase sent me back for more blood tests. I don't know exactly why because I haven't had a chance to talk to her."

"Okay, it doesn't mean cancer. It can mean a whole host of things, most of which are minor. Think positive." Karrington didn't reply. She'd heard that before from people who didn't experience the loss she experienced. "Look, where are you?"

"I'm almost home."

"I'll be there in a few. We'll have a couple of drinks and some dinner. How's that sound?"

"Good. Thank you, Olivia."

"You're welcome. On my way."

They hung up. Olivia could always be counted on to lift her spirits. Karrington hated always looking over her shoulder. She needed someone to talk to about her fears. After the case was over, she would seek out a good doctor to talk to. She pulled up in the driveway. This time Rich beat her home. She was glad. She walked inside and he was making dinner. "Wow, this is nice to come home, too."

"Well, my baby is busy with her big court case, so I decided to get home and make her some dinner."

"Aww, ain't you special?"

"All day you speak prim and proper. Then you come home to your southern roots."

Karrington giggled, "I can't help myself sometimes. Olivia is on the way."

"Okay, there's enough for two more... if she's bringing Maurice."

"I didn't ask. I'll call her now." Karrington whipped out her cell and dialed Olivia's number. "Hey O, are you on the way?"

"Yes, and a sister is hungry."

"You're always hungry."

"Okay, you got me there."

"Are you bringing Maurice with you?"

"Nope. Tonight is my night with my friend."

"Okay, that's cool with me." Karrington was happy she was alone. She needed to talk to Olivia about her blood tests. No matter how hard she tried, she couldn't help the nervous feelings inside of her. Every opportunity they got, they rose up in her. It wasn't good for her to be so anxious, but given the history of her family, she couldn't help it. We can talk alone when you're here."

"What are you going to do with Rich?"

"After he cooks and feeds us, he can go watch a game or something." They both laughed. "Seriously, this case is a drain on me. I need to recharge."

"I hear you. You got some wine?"

"Yes, and an extra bedroom, too."

Olivia burst out in laughter. "I can't believe you think wine will get me drunk."

"You shouldn't take a chance when you can stay here with me."

"Okay, I might take you up on it."

"Great. See you when you get here."

"Roger that."

Olivia and her military language. That was something new about her, but she understood it. After changing clothes, Karrington returned to the breakfast bar. From her barstool, she watched her husband make dinner. She loved a man who could cook. Rich was surprisingly good at it. She laughed at the thought that he was a better cook than her.

After a few moments Rich noticed her, "Hey, how long have you been sitting there?"

"Not long. I just wanted to admire your cooking. There's nothing better than a man who can cook. It's a bonus that looks good when doing it."

Rich chuckled. "Oh, sounds like it's going to be a great evening."

"Well, sort of… Olivia is coming for dinner."

"That's right, you said that. Is Maurice coming?"

"Nope, just Olivia." The couple made small talk until the doorbell rang. Olivia joined them. Karrington was happy to see her friend.

Rich's dinner was fabulous. The ladies enjoyed it, then retired to Karrington's home office to have wine and cheese. After a few hours of conversation, they each went to bed. Karrington was disappointed she didn't get to talk about her follow up blood tests. She didn't want to dim the conversation. Olivia was excited about her impending marriage. Karrington drifted off to sleep. She slept throughout the night.

The morning sun rose. Karrington went out to meet with her friend. "Hey, did you sleep well?" Olivia cut her eyes at her, then quickly looked away. She was obviously keeping something from her. "What's wrong Olivia?"

"Nothing, it's crazy… I need to get to work. I'm going to be late, and you know Uncle Sam don't play." She rushed to the door, leaving Karrington confused. Olivia turned, "I'll call you later."

"Okay, Olivia." She walked out the door. Karrington paused there for a moment, trying to understand what happened. She turned and Rich was behind her. "Do you know what's wrong with Olivia?"

"How would I know?" He held up his hands in an inquisitive manner. "You guys left me last night, remember?"

"Hey, I do." She pushed past him and headed to the bathroom to wash up and get dressed. On the ride to the courthouse, Karrington couldn't get her mind off Olivia. She tried to call her, but she didn't answer. Her cell rang. It was Dr. Chase's office. She answered, "Hello."

"Hi, this is Dr. Chase. Is this Karrington Lewis?" Dr. Chase never calls her. She felt her blood pressure rise. A knot in her throat prevented her from answering. "Hello?"

"Yes, this is Karrington."

"Hi Karrington, I got a message to call you."

Karrington remembered Angie told her she would have Dr. Chase get back with her. It was a sigh of relief. "Yes, I called about the follow up blood tests. Is there a reason for concern?"

"I'm afraid there is Karrington."

The answer stunned her. She was relieved that Dr. Chase was only returning her call, but now she knew it's bad news. "What's wrong?"

"Some of your numbers have me concerned, so I retested you. The results were the same. I need you to come in for an examination. There are several reasons that could explain the numbers. I want to examine you to narrow that down."

"It's cancer, isn't it?" The line was silent. "I can take it Dr. Chase."

"Look Karrington, I'm not going to pull any punches with you. It could be breast cancer. We're not sure yet. It could be other things too. We need to see what it is for sure before we determine how to treat it."

"I understand Dr. Chase. I'm in the middle of a big case, so I don't know when I can come in for an examination."

"What time is court usually over?"

"Four most days; sometimes five."

"Call my office and set something up for tomorrow at five. Tell them I authorized it."

"Thanks Dr. Chase."

"You're welcome. Karrington, we're going to beat this… whatever this is."

"I know Dr. Chase. Thank you."

"You're welcome."

The line went dead. Karrington's worst fear was coming to life. *How am I going to make it through court today? Lord, this can't be happening to me. I'm too young. Please don't let me die!* She parked in the courthouse parking lot. Her head dropped on the steering wheel, and she cried. Karrington didn't know how long she was there. Someone tapped on her window and startled her.

"Ma'am, are you okay?"

"Yes." She grabbed her bags and exited the car. "Thank you for checking on me, but I'm fine."

"No worries. That's what we're here for, ma'am."

Karrington was happy the guard interrupted her pity party. She needed to get strong for this case, for this day, and for her life. Telling Rich and Olivia would be the hardest thing to do. Karrington was happy she had a man who would stick by her and a best friend who would never leave her side. She couldn't imagine a life without them now. She arrived in court and took her seat. The day would be long and hard, and it would be enough of a distraction to help her forget about the upcoming bout with a demon known as cancer.

The day ended early, around three. Karrington went back to her office to tighten up the case. The defense would start the next day. Once in her office, she made her appointment with Dr. Chase. Dr. Chase was able to get her in that evening at five. *Should I tell Rich and Olivia before I meet with Dr. Chase? I don't want to, but something is telling me I should tell someone. I love them. I don't want to burden them with this if it turns out to be nothing. Hmm, there is someone I can call. She's a prayer warrior if ever I knew one. Hopefully, she's available. I really need her now.* She dialed Marlena Sutherland's number. Marlena and Karrington grew up together. Marlena lived in the church. She was a minister in her church in Maryland. Marlena picked up, "Hey Pastor, Minister girlfriend."

"Karrington Lewis… I mean Johnson! How are you, girl? I haven't heard from you in months."

"I know, and that's my fault. I should have checked in long before now. I won't allow that to happen anymore."

"Karrington, it's a two-way street. I should have checked in as well. So we're here now, on this phone. What made you contact me?" There was silence. Karrington didn't know how to bring it up. "I know something is wrong, Karrington. I've known you since we were in kindergarten. I know your signs, when you're happy, when you're sad, when you're in love… that was a new one from last year. Spit it out."

Karrington took a deep breath. She started to say the words, but they didn't come out, so she took another deep breath. "As you know, I have dealt with death and illness all my life. The Lewis women have suffered long and hard. Now it's my time. I have an appointment in an hour with my doctor, Dr. Chase. She's not sure yet." Karrington pauses. "She thinks I could have cancer. She wants to examine me, to be sure."

"Let's pray."

"Somehow I expected more."

"Karrington, God is more. When we turn our problems over to God, He handles them."

Karrington didn't respond. Prayer was the answer. So many Lewis women went on to be with God that she wasn't sure if she had enough faith to beat it. "Let's pray, honey."

"Okay."

"Father, my sister Karrington Johnson has been given a diagnosis. But Lord, that diagnosis is from man, not from you. Remind her Lord, that nothing happens in your world by accident. You are the author and finisher of everything. Touch not only her body, but her mind. Heal her of everything, including the cancer that may be inside her body. Lord, grant her the comfort to handle this situation with the strength of all those women who came before her. Surround her with people who will support her, give her the strength to exercise and eat right daily. Most of all, Lord, bless her with the knowledge that you are not a man and cannot lie. If we ask for healing, you will grant it. In your wonderful Son Jesus' name, Amen!"

"Amen, and thank you so much, Marlena. I really appreciate the covering."

"Any time, my friend… any time."

"I'm on my way to the doctor. I will keep you informed."

"Thank you and may God go with you."

"Amen. Bye Marlena."

"Bye."

Karrington hung up the phone, answered a couple of interoffice emails and headed to the doctor. She dreaded the appointment, but she knew it had to be done. The examination would tell her where she was and even if it was cancer.

The drive to Dr. Chase's office seemed longer than normal. She arrived at the office. No one was waiting in the outer office. Angie said, "Hi Miss Johnson. Dr. Chase is waiting to see you."

"Excellent."

"This way." Angie guided her to the room where she would take her vitals. "How is the case coming? It's all over the news."

"I know, which isn't good for my client, but all-in-all, it's going well. Tomorrow is my turn to put on my case."

"I'm sure you will do an amazing job."

"Thank you for the vote of confidence. I wish you were on the jury."

Angie smiled, but Karrington read the smile to say she wouldn't have sided with her client. She understood most women hated her client. His personality was one that endured women to love him unless he was trying to get with them. "Okay, Dr. Chase will be in to see you in a minute."

"Thank you, Angie."

"You're welcome."

Karrington waited in silence. She wanted to text Olivia but decided not to do it. She wanted this appointment behind her first. Tonight would be difficult for her. She hated that, considering tomorrow would be her biggest day in court. Dr. Chase walked inside the room and half smiled at her. The half smile told Karrington everything she needed to know. This would not be an appointment she would enjoy.

"Okay Karrington. I'm going to be straight with you. The signs are there for cancer. We aren't sure you have it. We need to do a quick examination, but I'm sure we will need to do a biopsy on you. We can do it right here in the office. Are you available Friday?"

"I can make myself available. I will tell the judge that I have a procedure that needs to be done."

"Okay, Friday at three. That work?"

"Yes ma'am."

"Okay, let me examine you."

Karrington held back the tears. She remembered when her mother had her first biopsy. When she came home, she was in tears. Her dad told her to get off the floor and fight for her life. Her mother did just that. The first fight was tough, but she didn't succumb to cancer. She beat it and unfortunately, she lost her parents in a car accident.

Karrington thought about closing her eyes during the examination. She didn't. She didn't want Dr. Chase to learn that she was slipping into a depressive state. Try as she might, she realized depression was setting in. Dr. Chase said, "I believe we have a lump on your left breast. The biopsy will tell us if it's something we need to worry about or not." Dr. Chase took her seat. "You can get dressed now and have a seat over here so we can talk."

Karrington did as she said. *Here goes this 'don't be down or depressed speech.' Too late, I'm already there, Dr. Chase.*

Dr. Chase took her hand. "You've been a patient of mine for a long time now. You will be a patient of mine for a much longer time. We will get past this. You are young and strong. No matter what the result is, you can beat this. You have to have the right mindset. I'm going to refer you to Dr. Johanna Willoughby. Dr. Willoughby is a psychiatrist, a very good one at that. In order to beat cancer, you need to be prepared to win the fight, not just to fight. If you don't think you can win, then you won't. Do you go to church?"

"Not as much as I should."

"Then get back into church. A connection with God is very important." Dr. Chase took a deep breath. "I feel I've known you long enough to go here with you. God is a necessary relationship in all things that we do. This, for all we know, could be happening because He wants you back in church."

Karrington pondered her words. Since her marriage, she had strayed away from church. Before her marriage, she got Rich into church. His world seemed to have pulled her out of church. "You might have a point, Dr. Chase. You can bet I will be back in church on Sunday."

"Good for you. I knew the Spirit wanted me to share that with you."

"I talked to my friend who's a minister today. She said it had been a while since we talked. That's because I haven't been to church. I will be there on Sunday. Nothing will stop me."

"Good for you. In the meantime, go to the gym—"

"Haven't been doing that either."

"Get some rest and eat right."

"I can say I haven't been doing those things either."

"Your victory starts today, young lady. I will see you Friday afternoon. Don't worry, God has you."

"Thank you, Dr. Chase."

Dr. Chase smiled at Karrington. Unlike Angie's smile, Dr. Chase's smile reassured Karrington that she was sure what she said was true. Dr. Chase believed God had Karrington. Karrington believed it now. *I may have this affliction, but I also have Jesus. Nothing will stop me from ringing that bell!*

6 – The Fight Begins

Karrington stopped at the light a few minutes from her home. She glanced to the side and recognized a car that looked like Rich's car. *Hmm, that looks like Rich's old car, but it was totaled. I guess someone else has one like him.* She pulled off, not giving it another thought. She pulled into the garage and there was a new car sitting there. *Rich must have finally got that car he wanted. It's about time.* She walked into the house. "Hey honey. I see you got a new ride. I love it."

"Yeah, I know you were tired of my rental, so I finally broke down and got one."

"It looks so good, too. When are you taking me for a ride?"

"Tonight. Maybe we'll drive down the 95 to Richmond and back."

"Wow, that's a long drive."

"Yeah, but it will be fun to get away."

She liked the idea of going on a quick road trip. She couldn't go unless she told him what was happening to her medically. Karrington wondered if she was not telling him because deep inside, she believed he would run off. The thought melted away when he took her into his strong arms and hugged her tight. She laid her head on his chest. It seemed to fit perfectly. It was moments like this that nothing else in the world mattered to her. She was in love with him. She gently pulled away. Karrington braced herself on the kitchen counter. "Honey, I have something to tell you."

"You didn't cheat on me, did you?"

She chuckled, "That would never happen."

"Okay, what you got?"

"I went to the doctor today. She wants to do a biopsy on me Friday at three."

"Okay, so what?"

"You aren't concerned?"

"No. Just because they do a biopsy doesn't mean you're sick. It could be benign for all we know." She smiled inside, loving the fact that he had confidence that she was fine. "Look, I deal in facts, not 'what ifs.' One fact that I know is that you're a fighter. Nothing will stop my baby. Now let's hit the road."

"In rush hour traffic? No, thank you. Maybe we should go Saturday morning when it's less traffic."

"Okay, what do you want to do tonight?"

"Watch a nice movie, eat some good healthy food and relax with my king."

"You got it, baby."

The Defense Begins

Karrington's day started at five in the morning. She wanted to take her doctor's advice before she had the biopsy. Hard as it may have been for her, she dragged herself out of bed, slowly went down to the basement and rode her bike for 30 minutes. Following that, she ran on the treadmill for another 30 minutes. She had a notion. Her Bible sat on her treadmill. Reading the Bible was a thing for her when she was hard in church. Lately she hasn't had time to read it. Now that would change. She flipped through it until she settled on a scripture her grandmother used to read during her battles. There it was, staring her straight in the face, Isaiah 53:5. *But he was pierced for our transgressions, he was crushed for our iniquities; the punishment that brought us peace was on him, and by his wounds we are healed.* Karrington held her head high. *Yes Lord, I feel your presence! I know you are here. This will not defeat me!* She bowed her head. *Father God, the weapon may form, but it will not defeat me, it will not prosper, it will not depress me; I will be victorious in your Son Jesus' name… Amen!* She clinched her fist and opened her eyes. Standing in front of her was her handsome husband, grinning. "How long were you watching?"

He raised his eyebrow. "About five minutes, but you certainly inspired me. I don't know what you said in your prayer, but I felt something inspirational."

"Well, I'm glad you did, Mr. Johnson. I won't let this beat me."

"This? We don't know yet, honey. Don't give it power over you."

"You're right. Nevertheless, I'm taking Isaiah 53:5 with me everywhere I go. Even after the results come back."

"What's that scripture?"

"Let me share it with you, babe. You should have it in your spirit, too. You're my husband and my strongest supporter, so you should know it too. She recited the scripture to impress Rich. "So, when you pray remember that scripture and remember your wife, fighting this battle."

"There is no battle. Don't give it power over you."

Karrington walked up to him. She placed her arms around him and laid her head on his chest. "I understand what you're saying. We have to be prepared, no matter what." She lifted her head off his chest and patted it. "Now, I have to get ready for this day in court. Pray for me." She left him standing where he was. He didn't answer, so she looked back. "Is there something wrong, Rich?"

"No. I just don't want to think about it." He dropped his head. "I don't want to lose you."

She rushed back to him and embraced him as hard as she could. "You will not lose me, Mr. Johnson. We will be together forever!" He hugged her back and laid his head on top of her head.

Karrington dressed and headed to the courthouse. She needed to be on her A game today. Making her case for her client was imperative. This was her first opportunity to show the partners in her firm that she could win the big case. Confidence in the courtroom was something Karrington never lacked. Her mind shifted to Olivia. *I haven't heard from my girl in a couple days now. I need to at least reach out to her and see what's up.* Karrington dialed Olivia's number, but it went straight to voicemail. *Something is definitely wrong. Is she blocking me?* Olivia returned her call. *Oh, she must have had it on vibrate.* "Hey O, where have you been?"

"Hey Karrington. I've just been busy at work and with Maurice. He's been really needy lately. I don't know what it is."

"You left my house in some sort of mystery and I still don't know what's going on." Olivia didn't respond. "Olivia?"

"Oh sorry, someone was handing me something. It was nothing Karrington. I just needed to get to work."

This doesn't sound like my girl. Something is up and she won't tell me. "Olivia, you know I know you better than that. Something is wrong and you're not talking to me. It must have happened in my house. Now if my husband hit on you or something—"

"No… God no, that's not what happened."

"Then tell me."

"I just don't want to talk about it now, Karrington. Can we please let it go for now?" Her voice was stern and straight to the point. "Somethings are not meant to be talked about right away."

"I understand Olivia." She didn't really understand, but Karrington didn't want to start a fight. She loved Olivia and whatever she's going through will come out later. "If you ever need to talk, you know I'm here."

"I know." An uncomfortable pause rested over the phone lines. "I'm sorry, Karrington. I don't mean to be harsh. I just need some time… okay?"

"I get it Olivia. Trust me, I understand when you need to be to yourself." She paused. "I hate to pile on, but I have a biopsy tomorrow."

"What? Why?"

"Dr. Chase suspects something, and she wants to check it out. After the biopsy, she'll run tests and know more then."

"Oh, my Karrington. I'm sorry I haven't been there for you."

"It's okay. I just found out yesterday."

"Can we do something tonight?"

"Rich and I are driving to Baltimore tonight. He has a new car, and we want to put it on the road. We were going to wait until Saturday, but he decided he wanted to do it tonight before the biopsy."

"I understand. Call me later… if you can."

"I will."

"Good luck on your case today. I know you're putting on your defense."

"Thanks Olivia. I appreciate it. I'm at the courthouse now, so I'll try to call later."

"Thanks, bye Karrington."

"Bye Olivia." Karrington hung up the phone. She wanted to know what was going on with Olivia. Rich claimed to know nothing, and Olivia said it wasn't about him hitting on her, so she wondered what it could be. She had to rid her mind of the issues in her personal life. This day was about defending her client. She was close to winning her first case. Nothing could distract her. She marched into that courtroom like she owned it, ridding the negativity of her personal life. Karrington's focus remained on the case and defending her client until the judge released everyone for the evening. The judge kept them longer, since Karrington had to leave early the next day.

She headed home to meet Rich for their drive to Baltimore. The trip really didn't excite her after a long day, still she didn't want to disappoint him. She pulled into the garage like she usually did. Rich's new car was still warm. She walked inside. Rich's voice was coming from the living room. He was arguing with someone. Karrington couldn't hear the other person. When Rich's eyes locked in on her, he quickly said, "I have to go." He hung up the phone. "Trouble at work."

"What do they want you to tell?"

"It's just work stuff, babe. Nothing you need to be concerned about."

"I don't like secrets. You're keeping secrets now, Olivia's keeping secrets, and it all started the night she was here. If you guys—"

"There's nothing going on between me and Olivia. I wouldn't date her if I was single and alone." Karrington's eyebrow raised. "I'm not saying she's not attractive. I'm saying she's not my type. Anyway, are we still going on the drive… you're home late."

"Your car is warm, you just got home too."

"Just before you. It really isn't a good day to take the drive."

"Yeah, I'm sensing that." She turned and walked to the bedroom. Karrington sat down. *Something is going on here. They both claim nothing is happening with them. I suspect each one of them has a secret.*

126

Rich never brought his work home before. Now he's arguing with someone about work. Doesn't sound right. I really don't need this now. My biopsy is tomorrow. I need to be calm and relaxed. I think I will reach out to Marlena. She's the best one to talk to at this point. Karrington got changed and walked back into the living room. Rich was consumed with the sports news network. "I'm going to see Marlena. I'll be back in a little while."

"I thought we would spend the evening together."

"Maybe you and Olivia should hang out." She knew her comment was wrong, but she felt the way she felt. Once in her car, she took a deep breath. She started the car and headed to the church to see Marlena.

There were several cars in the church parking lot. Thursday nights were choir rehearsal nights. Marlena often made an appearance since she was the minister who oversaw the music department. Karrington recognized her car. She went inside and Marlena was talking to someone near the door to rehearsal. She heard the music blaring from inside. It touched her spirit. *That's just what I need, a healing song. Thank you, Lord.*

"Karrington!" Marlena jogged toward her and hugged her. "I'm so happy to see you."

"I'm happy to see you Marlena… Minister Sutherland."

"Either will do, girl. Come on in my office." Marlena led her to the office around the corner. Inside it was nicely decorated with awards, degrees, and tons of books. "Have a seat."

"I forgot you were an avid reader."

"I love a good book! Have you read Broken Pieces? It's about grief and when I say it was good… girl, it was really good. You should check it out."

"I'm not big on reading much anymore, except case law and legal journals."

"You should squeeze in some recreational reading. It will help with your stress."

"Is it that obvious?"

"Yes, it is." She smiled at Karrington. "What can I do for you?"

"My life is falling apart. I'm winning my case, at least I think I'm winning. You can never be sure until the jury comes back. But my personal life sucks. I think my best friend is lying or hiding something from me. My husband is definitely lying or hiding something from me, and I can't help but think they are sleeping together."

"Oh, no! Please tell me that's not true."

"I only have my suspicions." She stopped talking and thinking she was telling too much.

Marlena said, "You don't have to be concerned that I will share what you tell me. This is

128

conversation by privilege. You know that better than anyone."

"I do. I'm just embarrassed."

"Don't be. Everyone has issues in this life. It may look to you they have it all together, but honey, looks can be deceiving."

"I invited Olivia to my house one evening. She stayed over. The next morning, I woke up, and she was in a hurry to get out of the house. I asked her what was wrong. She said she was late and just needed to get going. That was never like her. Since then, she's almost ghosted me. I rarely hear from her and when I do, it's a quick conversation. When I asked her point blank, she said nothing was wrong at first, then she said she just didn't want to talk about it. When I asked her about her and Rich, she denied anything was happening. Same with Rich. I know something is happening."

"Wow, that is a lot to take in."

"And to add to that, my biopsy is tomorrow. Things are not at a good point for me."

"I can see why you're stressed but honey, this is all a test. While you were talking, the first chapter of Job came to mind. I could picture Satan arriving in Heaven and God saying have you considered my servant Karrington. You know the story." Karrington nodded her head. "You are being challenged by Satan.

All of this is being put on you, but your faith in Jesus will get you through."

"Yes. Sometimes I need a reminder of that Marlena. I knew you were the right person to talk to."

"Anytime you need me."

"Is it possible for you to come to my biopsy tomorrow?"

"Rich isn't going to be there?"

"I never asked him."

"Okay, then I'll be there. Where and what time?"

"Dr. Chase's office. Here's her card. I wrote the time on it too."

"I will be there, Karrington."

"Thank you so much."

Marlena came from behind her desk and sat next to Karrington. "Honey, this won't be easy for you. The mounting pressures are going to be hard to deal with. You can handle it. Do what the doctor says."

"Can't God just heal me?"

"Then how would you get to know him better? Trust him in every situation. Doctors are placed on this earth to guide us. If we listen to them, then God does the rest." Karrington stared deep into Marlena's eyes. "Once I was like you. Faced with

130

cancer. I was stage two, but I was scared like you couldn't believe." Karrington's mouth dropped. "I hung in there and kept my faith. I come from a family of ministers, so they all prayed for me, kept me strong when I was weak. I made it and so can you. Surround yourself with positive people who believe in God and the power of prayer. You will testify to someone down the line."

"I didn't know you went through this."

"I did. I'm glad I saved my testimony until today for you." Karrington smiled and dropped her head. It would be tough, but now she had some encouragement to make it through. "Karrington, some of your friends and family will have to draw away. You can't have negative people around you. Keep those who are positive near you. Those who are negative will need to go."

"I will remember that, thank you." Marlena took her hand. She rubbed it, encouraging Karrington that everything would be fine. "I guess I need to go home to my husband." Karrington stood up. "Thank you for seeing me on short notice."

"Anytime, my friend. Anytime."

Karrington hugged her and walked away. She headed home.

Karrington sat on the side of her bed. Rich was in his den. She used to believe he was talking to old friends, watching sports, or lighting one of his cigars. She hated the smell and asked him several times not to light up in the house. The compromise is that he could do it in his den if he blocked the door. She wanted him to come to bed. However, she didn't mind the quietness either. Karrington's mind raced through all her problems. It also ran through what Marlena said. Having friends was never a problem. Having friends that would stick by through thick and thin was another issue. She counted Olivia in that number. Now she wasn't sure. Tomorrow would be a big day on two occasions. One, she would close her case and the other involved her biopsy. She prayed both would end in her favor.

"Hey love." Rich walked into the room, breaking her thoughts. "You're just sitting on the bed, honey."

"You look high. Have you been doing drugs?"

"No baby, I had some brandy, though. Maybe one too many shots… maybe." He laughed. "But I'm here now, so let's get busy."

"Rich… Rich—"

"Come on baby, give me some."

She resisted him. The smell of his cigars angered her, but she remembered her aunt talking about submission. She changed her mind and let him have his way. For the first time since they were married, she hated it.

Case Closed; Biopsy Begins

Karrington finished her closing argument, and the judge turned the case over to the jury. After talking to her client, she remained at the defense table, deep in thought. Part of her hoped the jury would come back right away, so they would finish before her procedure. The reality of that happening was nonexistent. Her procedure would occur in an hour. She rose and headed out the door. The judge and prosecution knew she would be unavailable for the decision if it were to come back.

Karrington arrived at Dr. Chase's office at 2:45. She received a text from Marlena saying she couldn't make it. Her sister was in a car accident. Marlena was in the emergency room with her. Karrington understood but questioned why God wanted her to be alone in this.

They were ready for her procedure when she got there. Dr. Chase understood Karrington's case and wanted to get her in and out as quickly as possible. Karrington laid on the table thinking nothing but the worst. She caught herself and focused on a beachfront view. *No matter what the results are, I'm going to take a vacation somewhere. A beach is a must! I need to relax and prepare for any fight I have on the horizon.* Dr. Chase walked in, and the procedure began.

Karrington woke up from her biopsy. She looked around the room. Dr. Chase sat at a desk, making notes on her computer. Karrington asked, "Am I done?"

"Hey there. Yes, you are done. Take some time, get yourself together. You can leave whenever you're ready."

What are the results?"

"Oh, it will take a week to find that out. Is your case over?"

"It's with the jury."

"Well, take the weekend and relax. Please don't stress over this. Enjoy your weekend."

"I have more things to be worried about."

"Did you call Dr. Willoughby?"

"No, I haven't had a chance yet."

"Call him."

"I talked to a minister, though. She's very good and a friend. She knows me better than most."

"Good, at least you're talking to someone." Karrington didn't respond. She concentrated on getting herself together. "You know, Karrington, I can help you with the medical part, but you need help with the mental part. Remember what I said, surround yourself with positive people, exercise, eat healthy and rest."

"I will Dr. Chase. Minister Sutherland said something similar." She hopped off the table. "I will make sure this weekend is filled with all of that."

"Good. I hope your case ends well for you."

"Thanks Dr. Chase. You'll let me know the results when you get them, right?"

"Absolutely. I'll call you personally either way."

"Thanks Dr. Chase. You're the best doctor in the world."

Dr. Chase smiled. "Thanks, Karrington."

Karrington walked out of the office. *Why not start the relaxing and positivity with a nice hot latte? It doesn't really fit the healthy part, but hey… I need some comfort.* She arrived at the coffee shop and ordered her latte. It arrived when the text arrived. The jury was back. She said under her breath, *Dang it, just my luck!*

"Excuse me?"

"Oh, you heard that?" She laughed. "I'm sorry. I got a text that the jury is back on my case. I can't enjoy my latte."

"I thought I recognized you. You're representing Tyre, right?"

Karrington leaned forward, "Yes." She didn't want everyone to know who she was. Karrington smiled and headed out the door. It took her 15 minutes to get to the courthouse. During the drive, she tried to enjoy her latte, but it wasn't working out for her. She left it in the car and headed to the courtroom. She entered. Her client sat at the defense table. The prosecution arrived shortly after Karrington. Everyone took their place. The judge walked in, and the bailiff called the room to order.

The Judge said, "Madam Foreperson, I understand you've reached a verdict."

"Yes, Your Honor."

"Please hand it to the Bailiff." The foreperson handed the paper to the Bailiff who gave it to the judge. "I have reviewed the verdict and find nothing legally wrong with it." He handed it back to the Bailiff who handed it back to the foreperson. "Madam Foreperson, how do you find the defendant?"

The Foreperson replied, "We find the defendant… not guilty." The courtroom exploded. Reporters quickly tried to get their story out while supporters of Tyre celebrated.

The Judge said, "Quiet in the courtroom." The courtroom returned to order. "If there is nothing else, the jury is excused, and this case is over."

The Bailiff shouted, "All rise."

Everyone rose. Once the judge was out of the courtroom, Karrington shook hands with Tyre. "Thank you, Miss Lewis, for your impeccable defense of me. I truly appreciate it."

"You're welcome, Tyre." She turned and walked through the line of media people trying to get a quote from her. She didn't want to give them anything. Instead, she headed for her office. Karrington knew the partners were waiting for the verdict. They would be waiting for her when she returned.

Karrington arrived at the office. The lights were out. *That's unusual. I would have thought they would be here to talk about the case.* She unlocked the main office door. She walked inside. Karrington nearly jumped out of her skin.

"Surprise!" Everyone shouted at the top of their lungs. They clapped and hugged Karrington with smiles, illuminating the office lobby. One of the legal techs rolled out a cake with congratulations on it. Brad stood in front of the group. He was the firm's managing partner. "Karrington Lewis, I am very proud of you. I knew when we offered you the position that you would bring success to this firm, but success on this level is… well, even I didn't expect it. Great job."

"Thank you, Brad. I appreciate it. I appreciate everything all of you have done to support me and this cake and surprise… well, it just knocks me off my feet!" For a moment, the problems that were mounting in her life seemed small. The firm recognized her work, and she was on top of the world.

Guy walked up to her. "Harold had a good feeling about you. You proved him right. That will go a long way in your career. Good job, Karrington. There's another party a week from tomorrow. I'll send you the details. You should be there on the heels of this victory. Your career will be elevated, maybe even partner."

"Thank you, Guy. I truly appreciate that." Guy nodded and walked away. *This day is turning out to be great for me. Praise God.*

The celebration ended, and Karrington headed home on a high. On her drive she blasted her music, tapping the steering wheel to the beat. At the light, she noticed a car next to her laughing at her. She waved at them and kept dancing to the tunes. Before she knew it, she arrived home. Karrington jumped out of the car and headed inside. Rich met her. They hugged. "Congratulations Karrington! We have to celebrate."

"What do you have in mind?"

"How about a nice dinner... in Mexico?"

"Mexico?"

"Yeah, we make good money. You're a lawyer who's on top of the world and I'm a biomedical engineer. We got six figure bank accounts, so let's spend some of it!"

Karrington didn't come from wealth. She desired to hold on to every penny, but this was a time in her life where she thought she should allow herself to live. "Okay honey, let's do it. Make the arrangements while I pack."

"Alright! Let's go."

Karrington rushed into the bedroom. She pulled out her suitcase. One job she assumed in the marriage was packing for the both of them. She learned what he liked to wear while traveling. Packing for both of them was easy for her now that they traveled a few times. Karrington returned to the kitchen. Rich finished making the arrangements. "We got tickets?"

"Yes ma'am. You got my shaving kit?"

"Of course, sweetheart, but remember you said, let's spend some of it. So… if you don't have something, buy it." She smiled, using his words against him.

"I said spend it, so hey… let's spend it!"

Cancun, Mexico

The couple headed toward the airport. They flew out of Reagan International. Their flight left at seven. They arrived in Cancun at one Saturday morning. Karrington was tired, so they went directly to the hotel. Once they settled in, Rich wanted to go out, but Karrington was more tired than she expected. She wondered if it had anything to do with her biopsy. "You can go ahead, Rich. I'm going to hit the sack. I'm tired."

"Okay honey. I won't be long. It's already two, so I'll just get the lay of the land."

"Okay." She kisses him. Rich left the room, and she got into bed.

The morning sun woke Karrington up. She looked at the time. It was eight. Rich laid next to her. *Wow, I didn't hear him come in.* She got up, looked out the window, and watched the people milling about. It was easy to spot the vacationers in the crowd. She chuckled at the thought she would be one of them later that day. Mexico was exciting to her. Getting into the experience would be fun. Karrington definitely wanted to experience the beach. Playa Delfines was the beach her co-workers recommended she visit. When Rich woke, she would drag him to there.

Karrington washed up and dressed. Rich was still asleep. *Okay, he's going to get his butt up so I can see Cancun.* She pushed his shoulder, waking him from his sleep. "Honey, you can't sleep the morning away. I'm ready to get out there."

"Okay, give me five more minutes."

"No, you shouldn't have stayed out all night." She folded her arms. Rich rolled over and sat up in bed. When she folded her arms, he knew she wasn't having it. "Where were you all night? What time did you come in?"

"I hit a club, and it was hopping until seven this morning."

"You knew I would get up. What did you think I came here for? I want to hit the beach."

"Okay, okay. I'm up and getting dressed. Last thing I need is you nagging me."

"Nagging you?" She stomped over to her purse. "I'll go by myself. Go back to sleep; maybe we'll meet up later." She walked out the door, hearing him plead his case. The door opened behind her.

"Hey, come on Karrington…" She didn't respond. "Come on, I'll be dressed in a minute."

"I'll be having breakfast in the restaurant."

"Okay, I'll be down in a minute."

She wanted to ignore him. The nagging comment riled her up. She didn't want to fight the entire time they were in Cancun. Relaxing and having fun was at the top of her list. Winning her first big case was a cause for celebration. Taking her mind off her medical issues and her best friend were secondary issues. Fighting with Rich was something she didn't want to do.

Karrington took a seat in the restaurant, which was in the hotel. The smell of the freshly cooked waffles tantalized her soul. She loved the smell and had to have them. She ordered the blueberry waffles. Karrington salivated at the thought of them. Out of the corner of her eye, she saw someone. Karrington looked, but the person moved behind a pillar. *Was that… it couldn't be. What are the chances?*

Rich joined her, "Hey, did you order already?"

"Yes."

He motioned for the server to come over and ordered waffles as well. "Come on, Karrington. Don't be mad at me."

"You said I was nagging you because I wanted to get out and see some sights. I mostly want to go to the beach. You didn't even dress for the beach. You see how I'm dressed, or were you too drunk to notice?"

"I'm not drunk." She noted he was visibly angry. "I had a couple of drinks. There were people down there having fun in the bar. I lost track of time and stayed out longer than I expected."

She huffed. "I'm not here to argue. Can we go to Playa Delfines?"

"Yes, I'll go change after we eat."

"Thanks."

After breakfast, Karrington waited on the street for Rich. She shopped at some stands, hoping to get an authentic dress for a good price. She could afford anything, but she truly wanted to help the Mexican people selling their wares on the street.

When she looked up, she spotted a woman she recognized from high school. Connie got into a cab and drove off. *Wow, I haven't seen her in years. It's odd that she's in Mexico at the same time as me.* Rich interrupted her thoughts.

"How you like me now?"

She chuckled. He was trying to make her happy after their argument that morning. "You… you look nice, husband. Guess who I just saw?"

"Who?"

"Connie Conley from high school."

"Wow, small world. What did she say?"

"Nothing. She got into a cab before I could catch up with her. Funny seeing her here." Rich nodded, staring at a vendor across the street. "Rich, are you listening to me?"

"Yeah babe. Funny seeing Connie here. You know we don't own the rights to who visit this country, right?"

"Funny man. I wonder if her bestie is here."

"Please don't start Karrington."

"Hey, I'm just asking. Connie and Diedre were besties. You didn't see one without the other one." Rich didn't respond. "Is she here Rich?"

"I don't know, babe." He rolled his eyes at her. Karrington didn't truly believe him. "Can we go to the beach and not argue again? Especially about something I can't control."

He's right. There is something funny here. Or am I overthinking this? He can't stop Connie or anyone else from visiting the country. It just seems odd that he picked the very place where Diedre's bestie is visiting. Maybe that woman this morning was Diedre. Something isn't right. I need to keep my eyes open. "Let's go honey." They caught a cab and headed to the beach. Karrington focused on the fun she was about to have. The water always made her feel better. *God knows I need the water now. I can't even come to Mexico and get away from issues.*

Once on the beach, Karrington's excitement increased. She found chairs for both of them, and they relaxed in the sun. Rich put sunblock on her, and she felt excited by his touch. *This man knows how to get me going. Oh Lord, I need to resist… until we get back to the room.* After relaxing on the beach, Karrington went for a swim, leaving Rich alone. Rich wasn't much of a swimmer, but Karrington loved the water. She dove in, allowing the water to cover her body. The feel of it caressed her. It was like no other feeling. All the negativity that once resided in her rolled away with the waves. She imagined them drifting off into the sunset, away from her.

After her swim, she noticed Rich at the top of the mound by the parking lot. He was in a deep discussion with a man Karrington didn't recognize. The man pointed at Karrington as she was drying off.

The look on Rich's face said he was busted. *I wish that feeling in the water could have lasted forever. I guess not. Soon as I'm out, it's right back to suspicion and deceit. This time I'm not even going to ask about it. I have to take care of myself.* Karrington sat back in her chair. Minutes later, Rich joined her.

Rich asked, "How was the swim?"

"Fine."

"Okay, not your usual celebration."

"Nope."

"You want to know who that was, right?"

"I'm done trying to figure out what you're doing, Rich. I just completed my biggest case, came down here to enjoy a mini vacation, relax from all my problems back in DC and attend to my health. All I seem to get is more suspicious acts from you. No, I don't want to know, nor do I care to know. From this moment on, I'm taking care of me." Karrington stood and headed for the parking lot. Rich followed her. She knew he didn't know what to say. Karrington never shut down like this with him before.

Rich hailed a cab, and they both got inside. "Let me make it up to you, honey."

"You mean again?"

"Yes, again."

"What you got for me this time, Rich?"

"Let's have dinner at Santana's. I hear it's one of the best restaurants in Cancun."

"Sí, lo es!"

Karrington asked, "What did he say?"

"I'm not sure, but I think he said, 'yes, it is.'"

"Well, he should know."

Rich asked the driver to take them to Santana's for dinner. "Honey, my co-worker said we have to try this restaurant. I'm hoping it's as good as he says."

"Me too, but what makes you think you can buy me off with food?" He tilted his head towards her. Karrington laughed. "Okay, I guess you know me." Karrington smirked as she got out of the cab. She was angry and suspicious, but she loved him. *I can only pray he's not deceiving me. In the meantime, let's eat!* Karrington followed the host to their seat. She scanned the menu while listening to Rich talk to the server about wines and the special for the day. Karrington wanted to stay in the beach arena, so she ordered the seafood special while Rich ordered a steak. Karrington laughed, "You come to a seafood restaurant to have a cow."

"Not just any cow, baby."

"Oh, okay."

"So Karrington, how are you feeling? You look a little tired."

Karrington didn't want to think about it. She hoped it was the sun draining her, but she knew deep inside it wasn't. The results hadn't come back. She grew increasingly tired all the time. She looked down and didn't want to respond. The server returned with a follow up question for their order, so she hoped it would distract Rich and he would drop the subject. It only delayed it.

"Honey, are you okay?"

Karrington forced a smile on her face. "Yes, I'm good. I'm a little tired, but I'm good."

"Don't think about those results. We will beat whatever tries to come our way."

For the first time, she felt joy in her heart. *Maybe he really is on my side. I shouldn't be so quick to judge.* "Thanks Rich. I really needed to hear that." She sighed. "No matter how much I try not to think about it, I do. I don't want to be a burden on anyone."

"Burden? You're my wife. You would never be a burden on me. We will fight it. Nothing will stop us." She forced another smile. "Hey, let's go dancing after this."

"I want to, but I don't know how much fun I will be." She watched his face drop. "Okay, I will go and we will dance, baby."

"Yes. That's the Karrington I married."

This time, she really smiled from her heart. She let her suspicions control her so much that she didn't see that he was trying his best. "Don't get out there making a fool of both of us, Rich."

"That's what fun is all about, baby." He smiled the biggest grin since they arrived in Mexico. Whatever happened during that conversation with the man at the beach it changed him back to the man she fell in love with. "I'm going to have a couple of drinks and dance, dance, dance baby!"

Karrington burst out in laughter. "Oh, no. I'm going to regret going with you."

The meal ended, and it was delightful to Karrington. Good food always made her feel better. They headed back to their hotel to freshen up and dress for the club. It was across the street from the hotel. Karrington finally felt that satisfaction of enjoyment on this trip. The suspicious actions of her husband aside, she was having a great time. She wasn't a club person nor danced much, but tonight she felt tired. However, she wanted to have fun with her husband.

After they dressed, Karrington and Rich headed across the street to the club. Inside, they took a seat and Rich ordered drinks for them. "Hey babe, let's hit the floor. This is my jam."

"Rich honey, every song is your jam." They left their seats headed for the dance floor. Karrington laughed at Rich's moves. Everyone loved him. She

148

remembered how he was always the center of attention in high school. That part of him didn't change.

They danced for two straight songs before Karrington couldn't go anymore. She went back to her seat, out of breath. Rich asked, "Are you okay?"

"I just need to rest."

"You think it's cancer, don't you?"

Karrington didn't want to answer. The last hours had been fun. The last thing she wanted to talk about was cancer. "Sorry, boo, I shouldn't have said anything."

"It's okay." She faked a smile and tilted her head. "I guess we should talk about it at some point. I don't feel right, to be honest. Something is wrong and I can't faith my way into believing anything else. It's there, and the battle is on. I just need to be strong."

"You will be. You're the strongest person I know." She faked that smile again. "I'll be right beside you, Karrington."

"Thank you."

"That is, if you stop faking that smile to me. I know you're down, but that's when me, your husband…" He moved to sit next to her in their booth. "Stands by you. I'll help you, baby. What do I need to do?"

149

"Dr. Chase said I need to exercise, eat healthy, and surround myself with positivity."

"We'll do that. You swam, and you had seafood, so you're on the way." He took her drink from her. "No more of this for you."

She giggled. "I don't like it, anyway. I would have preferred wine."

"You should have said something."

"I didn't want to hurt your feelings."

"Oh my goodness, come on, Karrington. You wouldn't have hurt my feelings."

"Okay then, can we go back to the room? I'm exhausted." Rich looked at the dance floor. "I can go and you can stay and have fun. I don't want to ruin your time."

"Hold on." Rich got up and walked to the DJ booth. He said something to the man and handed him some money. When he returned, he said, "We can go back after this dance."

The music slowed down and Karrington's favorite slow song bellowed out through the sound system. "The Art of Love" always made her cry. The first time she heard the song, she sat on her bed and cried tears of joy hearing the artist tell his story of his first love. Karrington laid her head on Rich's chest. She imagined a world with only them in it.

They returned to the hotel room. Karrington washed up and laid on the bed next to a sitting Rich. He was eager to get back in the club. Her condition held them back. Karrington felt bad about it. She wanted him to enjoy himself and not worry about her. However, she wanted him to be there with her. She broke down and said, "Rich, you don't have to sit here and babysit me. I'll be fine."

"No, honey, I need to be by your side."

"You have been. I'm just going to go to sleep. Go enjoy yourself. What time is our flight tomorrow?"

"We leave at five in the afternoon."

"Oh good, so we'll have more time to do some things tomorrow. Go and have fun."

He turned and faced her, "Are you sure? I have no problem staying here."

"I'm fine. I am not so bad that I can't take care of myself."

Rich smiled. "You're the strongest person I know."

"I'm not sure about that, honey." He smiled again, then kissed her on the lips. He gathered his phone, then left for the club. Karrington got up and looked out the window. She wanted to see him walk over to the club. Minutes later, he came into view. Rich bounced around like he was a kid in a candy store. She smiled, knowing her permission made him happy. She returned to the bed and slowly drifted off to sleep.

Monday Morning Blues

After another day in Mexico, then the return trip back, Karrington could not get out of bed. *I'm clearly tired, a major symptom of this breast cancer. God, when will those results be back? I really need to know, but I'm going to follow Dr. Chase's instructions. Since I'm not working today, I'll go to the gym and eat right. I'll find the healthiest food I can and consume it.* Staying true to her word, Karrington finally crawled out of bed. She headed to the gym to get a good workout. *I should have stayed home and did my workout. But I probably wouldn't have done it. Here we go gym. God, give me the strength.* She hit the gym door and the employees all smiled at her.

One of them said, "Hey, you're the attorney that got Tyre off last week, right?"

"That would be me."

"Cool, you come to our gym. That's awesome."

Karrington laughed and said, "What would be more awesome is if I came here more often. I need to get my workouts in more."

"Hey, we're always here, ma'am."

"Thank you." *'Ma'am', oh my God, am I looking that old? He's just being polite, I guess. Well, treadmill I'm*

152

Karrington Johnson. Today, I will defeat you. She chuckled to herself. Karrington got on the treadmill and started her walk. Five minutes into it she wanted to quit, except she knew she had to fight for her life. Her mother and grandmother beat cancer without working out, so she wanted every advantage. *God, don't give me anything, let me earn it. 'Faith without work is dead.' I'm willing to put in all the work!*

After a grueling workout, Karrington headed home with a bottle of water in hand. She pumped up the music in her car to keep her spirits up. Her cell rang, interrupting her jam. "Hey Olivia, long time no hear."

"Yeah, you win a big case and be out. A sister don't hear nothing from you."

"Come on, girl. You know that's not on me. You were acting funky."

"Yeah, I'm over it. I miss my girl, though."

"Are you ready to talk about it?"

"Can we just chalk this one up and forget about it? I really don't want to go back there."

"Okay. Well, I'm headed home from the gym. Do you want to connect later?"

"The gym? Who is this?"

"Ha, ha. I can work out, you know. I have to."

"Your test came back?"

"Not yet, but I have not been feeling myself, so I'm getting ahead of the game. You know, proactive and all."

"Nothing wrong with that. Start going in the evening and we can go together."

"I can do that some days. Some days Rich wants to go with me."

"You mean he's down for helping you?"

"Of course. He's my husband."

"Hey, you never know until the rubber meets the road."

"Okay… yes, my husband is here for me."

"Okay, well let me know what days we can go. I'll work your butt off."

"Oh, you got jokes."

"I may be in the Air Force, but we work out."

"Okay, I'm sure you will be a definite help. I'm home now, so I need to hit the shower."

"Okay, have a great day in the Lord, Karrington."

"You do the same." Karrington hung up the phone. *Wow, it was so good to chat with my girl again. Today is a great day! I'm going to shower and relax, then eat me a salad. It's got to be something good, though. I can't hang with just a plain salad.* Karrington hit the shower and got into some relaxing clothes. She made herself a big salad with all the healthy items she could think of in it. She sat on the couch to eat. *Hmm, this is actually good. Who knew oil and vinegar dressing would accent these vegetables so well. I need this in my diet more often. Not too much though, so I don't get tired of it.* After Karrington finished her salad, she laid on the couch watching the news. They were talking about her client and his plans for the future. She dozed off.

"Honey… honey!"

Karrington felt a hand shaking her. She looked up at Rich. "Hey, when did you get home?"

"About 30 minutes ago. Are you okay?"

"Yes, I went to the gym, fixed myself some lunch and I must have dozed off. What time is it?"

"It's 4:30."

"What? I've been sleeping that long?"

"I guess so."

Karrington jumped up. She looked at her phone. "Oh, I have a call and a few texts."

"Anything good?"

"Just people congratulating me on the case. One voicemail from Dr. Chase, though." Rich came and sat by her while she played the message. It was not the news she was hoping for. Dr. Chase's message requested Karrington to come in so she could explain what her grade two results were in person. She set an appointment for the next morning. A pit in

Karrington's stomach formed. Rich put his arm around her. The facet of tears opened. Karrington couldn't contain them any longer.

"Baby, I am here for you. Whatever you need, I will be by your side." She was happy to hear that. She laid her head on his chest. Something she loved doing. "I'm going with you tomorrow. I want to hear from the doctor, too."

Through her tears she said, "Thank you." Olivia called her phone. Part of her wanted to answer, but she didn't know if she could handle it. She let it go straight to voicemail.

Rich asked, "Why didn't you answer?"

"I can't right now. I can't talk about it. Can you hold me until I stop crying?"

"I'll hold you as long as you need me to." Rich pulled out his phone and typed a text with one hand. He held the screen away from Karrington. She couldn't see what he was texting.

"Who are you texting? Are you telling them about me?"

"I had a meeting with some of the fellas about an investment. I'm telling them I can't make it. They don't need the details."

"Okay Rich. What time is the meeting?"

"Seven."

"You can go Rich. I'll be okay.

156

"No, I want to be here with you."

"Go. I can use the time to call Aunt Lisa and Olivia." She looked into his eyes. "Go."

"Okay, I'll be back as soon as it's over."

"I know you will." Rich went to the bedroom to change. Karrington sat on the couch in her sweatpants and tank top, wondering how much time she had left on earth. Her grandmother beat cancer three times. *Do I have it in me to do the same? Can I beat this?* She needed something to take her mind off her impending battle against a force she could not see or hear. Karrington pulled out her Bible and read it. *I'm going to simply open it. Lord, guide me to what I need to read for encouragement.* Karrington closed her eyes and opened the Bible. The Bible opened directly on Job 1:1. Karrington smiled. *Are you telling me I'm a righteous woman and that Satan has permission to bring this evil to me? Okay God, I accept that. Let the test begin!* Karrington dozed off with the Bible resting on her lap.

The same hand awakened Karrington shaking her. She opened her eyes. Rich said, "Come on honey, get in the bed with me."

"Are you trying to seduce me?"

"You're tired baby. You need your rest."

"Maybe… maybe not."

"Did you make the phone calls?"

"I did. I hate people feeling sorry for me. My grandmother used to say that all the time, 'Don't feel sorry for me!' Now I understand exactly what she felt."

"Come on, baby. Lay back down." She complied. Karrington reached up, grabbing his belt to pull him down to her. He obeyed. "You need to rest, sweetheart."

"I'm not paralyzed!" Rich huffed, then unbuckled his belt. Karrington's frustration grew. "Never mind. The mood is gone now." She rolled over in the bed and went to sleep.

Office Visit With Dr. Chase

Karrington was still angry at Rich from the night before, but she was happy he accompanied her to the doctor. It was nice having her husband by her side. They sat in Dr. Chase's office, waiting for her to arrive. Rich said, "Honey, I'm sorry about last night. I just wanted you to—"

"Forget it, Rich. It's over and done with." She refused to set her eyes on him. "All I wanted was a little love. Is this how it's going to be? You're going to truly act like I have a disability?"

"No. I'm sorry but—"

"Good morning. How are the Johnsons doing today?" Neither of them answered. "Okay, let's begin. Karrington, by your husband's presence, I'm guessing you are okay discussing your medical condition with him present."

"I am."

"Okay. You are stage two cancer. Before you get riled up, let's talk about that stage. The medical book's answer for stage two defines cancer cells as larger tumors that have grown more deeply into nearby tissue. In this stage, the cancer may have spread to the lymph nodes, and not to other parts of the body. In your case, they have not spread to your lymph nodes. However, this stage is not considered advanced cancer." Dr. Chase looked at the two of them. "Any questions?"

Karrington answered, "No, I'm familiar with it."

"I'm not. What can we do to fight this? My wife is not going to die, is she?"

"No, she isn't Mr. Johnson." Dr. Chase frowned. "I've explained what Karrington can do to help. Exercise daily, eat right, and surround herself with positivity. My suggestion for stage 2 can be treated with surgery—a lumpectomy and radiation treatment afterward. During the surgery, I will check the nearby lymph nodes for cancer. I want to make sure the results are accurate and the margins are clear. Afterwards, we will see what medications I will need to prescribe. Be prepared for chemotherapy. The object here is to reduce the chance of the cancer coming back."

Karrington said, "I understand. When can we do the surgery?"

"Wait, hold up. I need to understand this." Rich squirmed in his seat. "She's going to need surgery and radiation. How long will all of this take until she's healthy?"

Dr. Chase frowned. "Are you seriously asking that question? Do you know how sensitive this situation is?"

"I do." He looked back and forth between Dr. Chase and Karrington. "This is hitting me like a ton of bricks."

Dr. Chase said, "I understand, Mr. Johnson. Your wife needs you. She can get through this. She needs you, her family, and her best friends."

"I'll be here." He looked at Karrington. "I'll never leave your side."

Karrington smiled outside. Inside, she thought, *He's saying all the right things outwardly, but my gut is telling me something different. I can't escape it.* "When are we going to do the surgery?"

"I can schedule it for Friday. In the meantime... please do the things I asked you to do."

"I will Dr. Chase. Thank you for everything."

"You're welcome."

Karrington rose. She headed out the door, never looking behind her. She felt Rich's presence following her. When they reached the car, he opened the door for her. She stepped inside. He joined her. "Is there something wrong, baby?"

She rolled her eyes at him. *He didn't just ask me that ridiculous question, did he?*

"Besides the obvious, honey." He settled into his seat and started the car. "Can we get some breakfast?"

"I need to get to work."

"Baby, I didn't do anything wrong, did I? I'm here for you. I just wanted to know everything about this. You can't blame me for being worried. You're going under the knife."

She heard his words. Part of her realized she was taking the bad news out on him. It wasn't his fault this was happening to her. He was the easiest to take it out on. She turned to him. "I'm sorry. I'm clearly taking this out on you. I have to find a way to handle this news. Cancer has surrounded my family for years. I never expected it to rise in me at this young age. I feel like I'm being cheated out of my life."

He took her hand. "You will beat this… we will beat this."

His reassurance helped to settle her spirit. She looked at him. "We can have a quick breakfast." She looked at him. "Some fruit and decaf coffee?"

"Sounds great, baby. I know just the spot."

"Thanks, Rich."

The drive to the restaurant was quick. There were no words spoken between them. Karrington believed Rich was taking it in as much as she was. Although she had been through it before with her mother and grandmother, it was different when the focus was on her. She was afraid, yet faithful. *How can I have both emotions at the same time? This is the weirdest feeling. God, I'm trusting you to remove all that is not of you, including this cancer. Heal me Lord… heal me.* They arrived at the restaurant. Breakfast was good. Karrington didn't realize how much she would enjoy a simple breakfast with fruits and wheat toast. She was used to a hearty breakfast of eggs, bacon, toast and her favorite grits. Today, she needed to change her life. She had the faith to get through this, but could she do it alone? She didn't know. Karrington hoped she wouldn't have to find out.

Karrington arrived at work. She settled in to work to keep her busy for the day. With an unleashed power she had never experienced before, she worked. Before she knew it, the day was over. In fact, her end time had passed by two hours ago. She quickly gathered her things and headed out the door. Her car was home since Rich dropped her off, so she called a ride share to pick her up. Rich texted her several times, but she didn't answer.

The ride share dropped her off in front of her house. She unlocked the front door and walked inside. Rich wasn't home. She looked at his last text. He said he was hanging with the boys. He would be home around seven. Olivia texted her, too. She called Olivia back. "Hey Olivia, you called earlier?"

"I did. I was checking on my girl."

"I'm okay, I guess."

"You guess?"

"I need you, Olivia. Can you come see me?"

"Sure. I'm on my way now. Give me about half an hour."

"You got it." They hung up the phone. Karrington looked at the time. It was almost seven. She expected Rich would be home soon, but she didn't want to talk to him. She wanted him by her side, but somehow it didn't feel right to her. Something ate at her soul. The doorbell rang. Karrington opened the door. Olivia raced inside and hugged her tightly. "Oh my, I missed you too, my best friend!"

"I know I said 30 minutes, but I wanted to get here. I missed you, boo!"

"I missed you, too. Want something to drink?"

"Water is fine."

"Cool. Bottle or glass?"

163

"Bottle is good." She sat at the breakfast bar. "What's the update? You went to the doctor today, right?"

"I did." Karrington pretended to be busy getting the water, but in actuality, she didn't want to answer. She sighed, realizing Olivia deserved an answer. "She recommended surgery to remove the tumor... cancer."

"Okay, we can do this."

"I love your spirit."

"We've been through a lot, girl. I'm here."

"You know, I don't doubt it one bit, but when Rich says it... it just doesn't feel the same. I wonder, is it me or what?"

"Well, I have—"

The garage down opened. Rich walked inside. Karrington looked at her phone for the time. "You said seven. I guess you got held up."

"You know the boys. Everybody got something to say when you're trying to leave."

Karrington didn't believe a word he was saying. "I was just telling Olivia about the surgery on Friday."

"Friday? You left that part out."

"Sorry, I was getting there."

Rich opened the refrigerator. "Nothing to eat."

"I just got home, Rich."

"I'll order us something. What you guys want?"

Olivia answered, "How about Greek?"

Rich replied, "I can go for that."

Karrington chimed in, "It's good with me."

Rich responded, "Good, I'll order now."

Rich walked away. Karrington watched him walk away. "I don't know if it's me or not. Something is off. We're not clicking. I also can't help but wonder if you're hiding something from me."

Olivia stood, "I think you have enough to worry about. Rich is here, and that's a plus. I'm here too. You have your husband and best friend beside you. I'm sure Aunt Lisa will be there for you, too." She patted Karrington on the shoulder. "I have to hit the latrine."

"This isn't the Air Force girl." Olivia laughed, leaving Karrington at the breakfast bar. *Maybe it's me. I need to stop thinking people are doing something against me. Rich is here for me; I need to stop it and trust him.* Rich rejoined her at the breakfast bar. She stroked his cheek. "Thank you for ordering the food for us. I didn't even think about it on the way home."

"It's okay. I'm here to take care of you." Karrington smiled. Rich kissed her on the lips. The kiss excited her. Her spirit boiled with love. In a few seconds, she remembered falling in love with him.

"Oh, get it on y'all."

Karrington broke free of Rich. "I forgot you were here."

"I bet you did." They all laughed. "How long before the food, Rich?"

"It said 30 minutes."

"Okay, I guess I can hold out that long."

Karrington added, "Me too."

The group made small talk until the food arrived. Their small talk continued while they ate. Rich's phone beeped several times until he turned it off. Karrington asked, "Is someone dying to talk to you?"

"It's the group. They're planning a trip to see the game on Saturday. I told them I can't go. I'll be taking care of my wife, post op."

"That's sweet of you, honey."

Olivia chimed in, "I'll be here. If you really want to go."

Rich rolled his eyes at her. "There's no game more important than my wife."

"Okay, I was just offering."

"Look at y'all fighting over who's going to take care of little old me. I'm not incapable of taking care of myself post op or any other time." She looked at Rich, "If you really want to go, then go. I will not be the reason you don't get to live your life."

"You are my life."

The comment threw Karrington back. Her mouth hung wide open. "That was the nicest thing you have said about me, Rich Johnson. I don't know what to say."

"Oh, you know what to say, girl. You just don't want to say it in front of me."

"Get your nasty behind out of here." They burst into laughter. Karrington enjoyed the banter for the rest of the evening. She was having a good time, even though she was sick. Just what the doctor ordered.

7 – Surgery

Karrington woke up from her surgery. Rich sat in a chair next to her bed. He was fast asleep. Karrington's breasts burned with pain. She looked at them. Her face cringed. *He'll never look at them the same again.* She dropped her head against the pillow. Olivia came into the room. She noticed Karrington was awake. Karrington forced a smile through the pain and waved at her.

A technician followed. "Hi Miss Johnson, how do you feel?" Karrington's face frowned as she tried to raise up. "No, no honey, you need to relax a bit."

"It hurts… I'm just trying to get comfortable."

"We can give you something for the pain, but frankly, it's going to hurt for a while. It usually takes two weeks to recover." She tucked Karrington into the bed. "We'll get you written instructions on how to care for yourself. Do you have someone who can help you with your daily activities?"

"My husband… who's fast asleep over there."

"And me, I'll be there every day to help."

The nurse looked at Olivia. "Good, she'll need the help over the next two weeks."

Karrington asked, "What about the shape and size? Dr. Chase said they could do something about it."

"You would have to discuss that with her. I'm just a technician. I'll get her for you."

"Thank you." The technician left the room. Karrington looked at Olivia. "He will not like them anymore."

"If he loves you, he'll adapt."

"You don't believe that yourself." Rich shifted his weight in the chair. Karrington thought he heard them. His eyes opened and locked in on Karrington. "At least you stayed by my bed and slept."

"I didn't realize I dozed off. It has been a long day."

"It has."

"It will be a long recovery too," said Olivia. "But... we will get you through it."

Olivia took Karrington's hand. "I will come by every day. I'm working the night shift for the next few weeks. I'll come by during the day and Rich will cover the evening. We got you."

Karrington looked at Rich. "That's good with you?"

"Of course it is. I'm happy Olivia is here to help."

"That's good. I'm lucky to have you both."

Olivia said, "Blessed."

"Yes, I'm blessed to have you both."

Karrington cuddled into her bed. She closed her eyes, not wanting to discuss it anymore. She felt the tension between them every now and then. It could be the mounting thoughts of her fight against cancer. Something was off between them. Winning this battle had to be of utmost concern for her. She couldn't allow their squabble to interfere with that. Before long, Dr. Chase came in and gave her the instructions for caring for herself. She listened and looked at the list. *There's no way Rich is going to help me with some of this. Olivia will be in charge of helping me change my dressing and keeping the area clean. He'll be disgusted with the disfiguration. I can only hope I get some of that back. I can't let him bathe me. God, I wish Olivia could stay all day.* Dr. Chase finished and told Karrington the pathologist would let her know if there was cancer at the edge of the tissue she removed. Karrington prayed there wasn't. She wanted this to be over as soon as possible. It was in God's hands.

Back Home – Post Op

Karrington, Rich, and Olivia arrived at the Johnson home. Karrington laid on the couch while Rich made dinner. Olivia sat beside her. "Is there anything I can do for you, Karrington?"

"Go be with Maurice."

"Girl, he can wait."

"No, thank you for being with me during the surgery. Now it's time to go be with your man. Rich is here and Aunt Lisa is coming over. They got me."

"Okay, but only if you're sure."

"I'm sure." Karrington smiled. She didn't want to be the holdup with Olivia spending time with Maurice. "Go ahead."

"I'll call you later and check on you."

"Sounds good." Olivia grabbed her purse and went into the kitchen. Karrington didn't hear anything coming out of there. She hoped they were okay. She asked, "Olivia, are you still here?"

"Yeah, I'm still here." The look on her face was anger. Karrington suspected they were arguing about something. She hoped it wasn't about her care. She didn't like people having to wait on her. Olivia said, "I'll call you later."

"Okay, have a good time with Maurice."

Olivia smiled. "I will."

"Oh, what was that look about?"

"I actually miss him. Can't wait to see him."

"Girl, get out of here."

"I'm out." She opened the door. "Hey, here comes Aunt Lisa."

"Cool, shift change." Olivia laughed. Karrington heard them exchange pleasantries. Aunt Lisa walked inside and closed the door. "Hey Auntie. How are you?"

"How am I? The question is, how are you, baby?"

"I'm in some pain, but otherwise I'm okay. The doctor said it could take two weeks for me to heal and hopefully there's no more cancer."

"Prayerfully. Momma had that procedure before. The last time the cancer continued to spread." That's not something Karrington cared to hear. "But I shouldn't be sharing that with you because that's not going to happen to my niece You best believe that!"

"Thank you, Aunt Lisa."

"What's smelling so good in that kitchen?"

Rich shouted from the kitchen, "One of our favorite dishes! There's enough for you too, Aunt Lisa."

"Thank you, honey."

After dinner, Aunt Lisa left for the evening. Karrington moved to the bedroom. She fell asleep quickly. The discomfort from the surgery caused her to wake up at one in the morning. Rich hadn't made it to bed. Karrington hated that tugging feeling in her breast. Dr. Chase said it was common, but that reassurance didn't help her discomfort. After making her way to the bathroom she returned to the bed. She grabbed her phone and texted Rich but got no response. She laid in bed for a minute hoping he would respond, but he didn't. The garage door startled her. *He left me here alone. Tell me this man didn't just do that.* She eased her way into the kitchen where the garage door was located. Rich stood at the breakfast bar. *He doesn't look like he went anywhere.* "Where did you just come from?"

"What are you talking about?"

"I heard the garage door."

"Oh, I threw the trash out. I wouldn't leave my honey alone." He walked up to her and hugged her with a big smile.

"Be careful with the hugging," Karrington whispered.

"Are you feeling okay?"

"No, I have some pain in my armpit. It's not bad and Dr. Chase said that was normal. I also have some discomfort in my breast. Feeling like something is tugging at it."

"She said that was normal too, right?"

She glanced up at him. "Yes. You were paying attention."

"When it comes to my baby, of course I'm paying attention."

173

Karrington didn't know if she was aggravated or not, but Rich was annoying her. She reasoned it was probably the aftermath of the surgery. "I'm going to lie back down. Are you coming with me?"

"Yes, baby. I'm tired myself." They walked into the bedroom. "Aunt Lisa seemed to love the linguini."

"Yes, she loves Italian food. You can cook, so she probably would enjoy anything you make."

"Thank you, sweetheart. It's one thing my mother impressed upon me is to learn how to cook."

"She did well. Good night, Rich."

"Good night, honey."

More Bad News

The weekend progressed without much happening. Karrington's family and friends converged on her, making her feel happy. Love surrounded her from all angles, and it did her heart well. The rift between Rich and Olivia continued. It bothered Karrington. Neither one of them would not tell her what was going on. Both stressed that she shouldn't stress herself about their growing disagreement, still Karrington wanted to know why. She was bound and determined to find out.

Karrington arrived at Dr. Chase's office for her first radiation therapy treatment. She recommended External Beam Radiation Therapy for

Karrington. It all sounded like Greek to her, but she trusted Dr. Chase. Rich drove her to the office and sat with her while she waited for them to see her. Karrington wanted to ask Rich again about Olivia, but the time wasn't right. Instead, she picked up a copy of The Lyfe Magazine from the magazine rack and read through it. She said to Rich, "They have some great books and music reviews in here. Have you read this magazine?"

"I read it once or twice, but it's too nice for me. I need to read something with dirt in it. Tell me something behind the scenes. You know, who's sleeping with who or who's lying about their education, something like that."

Karrington rolled her eyes at him. *Who have I married?* "You know, people get tired of that kind of mess. It's refreshing to read about people doing positive things for the community."

"Yeah, I like a good mixture. I like to read about a good fight between the stars sometimes, you know."

"No, I don't." They called Karrington's name, and she rose to go back for her treatment. "Here I go, honey."

"You got this Karrington."

She headed back thinking; *He didn't even wish me luck. Does he hope some dirt will come of this?*

After Karrington's treatment, she returned to the waiting area. Rich popped up and took her by the arm. The tech said, "We'll see you tomorrow, Miss Johnson."

"Thank you." Karrington dreaded this daily treatment. "We're going straight home, right?"

"Yes."

"Good. I need some rest."

"I know, baby. I've canceled everything on my calendar."

"What about work?"

"I'm off this week and next."

"You know, Olivia said she could come by. She works at night."

"I'm your husband. I got this."

Karrington didn't know what to make of his comment. The last few days he'd been there, but not there for her. Now he's all in, taking off work and canceling all of his events. *Maybe Lord, he's coming around. Thank you for that.*

They made it home. Karrington sat on the side of the bed and flipped on the television. Rich made her lunch. "My stomach feels a little nauseous. I've only had one treatment so far and now I don't feel like I can eat."

Rich picked up the sandwich. "I don't know why not. Could it be a side effect?"

"Probably." I'll eat it anyway to keep my strength up. She finished eating. "I couldn't enjoy it, although I ate it all. I'm sure it was good, honey." She slides down into the bed. "I'm going to take a nap."

"Okay. I'll be in the living room. Text me if you need me."

"Okay Rich, thanks." Karrington laid down again. It wasn't long before she drifted off to sleep. Only a few minutes went by before mumbling from the living room woke her. She strained her ears to hear what Rich was saying. Karrington didn't hear another voice, so she reasoned he was on the phone with someone. Karrington listened as closely as she could. She couldn't hear much, but it sounded like he was arguing with someone about not coming to an event. *Why would someone argue with him about staying home to take care of his wife?* She wanted to go into the living room, but a strong urge to throw up came upon her. She rushed to the bathroom to take care of it. *God, these side effects are not going to be easy for me. Lord, I need your help. I can't fight this and be stressed about Rich at the same time. Open my eyes and allow me to see what's going on.*

Karrington rose. Rich stood behind her. "I heard you on the phone. It woke me up."

"I'm sorry, babe. Can I do anything?"

"No… well, hold me?"

"You know radiation will make you vomit, right?" He hugged her.

"I know that, Rich. Who were you arguing with?"

"Nobody. It was about work." Karrington didn't believe him at all. "Let me help you back to bed, baby."

"I can walk. I'm tired and my stomach is queasy, but I can walk." Karrington walked back to the bed and sat on the side. She asked, "Are you sure you want to go through this with me, Rich? The journey could be long and hard on you. I had to stand by my mom and my grandmother. I know you want to be out there partying. I don't want to hold you back."

"You're not holding me back. You're my wife."

"I can't help but think something is going on. Your actions are not lining up with your words. That phone call wasn't about work."

"Are you serious, Karrington? I've been a good husband to you. Why would I lie?"

"To cover up the truth, Rich."

"I'm not going to stand here and take this. I'm doing all I can for you."

"You are helping me. I appreciate your help, but you're hiding something too, Rich."

"You know what… Aunt Lisa said she would be here soon. I'm going out for a drink." He didn't wait for her response. He stormed out of the bedroom. Karrington jumped when the door slammed.

I guess he's mad. I had to ask the question. She grabbed her stomach and rushed back to the bathroom. Karrington closed the toilet seat and laid her head on top. *I knew this fight would be long, Lord. I know you're here with me. I don't know what's going on with my husband. I'll leave that for you. He says all the right things, but I don't think he wants to be here with me. I'm alone as I expected I would*—Her doorbell rang. Karrington got the strength to get up and answer it. It was Olivia and Aunt Lisa. "Hey guys. Aunt Lisa, I expected you, but Olivia, I didn't expect you."

"You look tired, girl," answered Olivia. "Let's get you somewhere off your feet."

Karrington took a seat on the couch. Aunt Lisa said, "Where's your husband?"

"He got mad and left."

"What? Let me call his behind right now!" Aunt Lisa stormed off toward the bedrooms.

Olivia sat down by Karrington. This could not go on for Karrington. She needed to know what was going on between Olivia and Rich. She asked, "I need to know what the problem is with the two of you. Tell me Olivia."

"I'm assuming you mean me and Rich." Karrington tilted her head, sending the message of 'really' to her best friend. "Karrington, just forget it. You need to focus on healing. Nothing else needs to matter." She took Karrington's hand. "Aunt Lisa and I will be here for you every day. Believe that!"

"I believe that. What's going on Olivia?" Olivia sighed. Karrington wasn't going to avoid the issue any further. "It all started the night you stayed here with us. Did he try something?"

"You're kidding right? He knows better."

"Then what Olivia?"

Aunt Lisa returned to the living room. "He wouldn't answer his phone. I'm sure he knows it's me calling."

Karrington replied, "He has caller ID. So yes, he knows. He's avoiding my calls, too." Her gaze returned to Olivia. "Tell me."

"The argument is over him telling you something you should know. I shouldn't tell you. He should. Hopefully, he will come through that door and we both will make him."

"He's had his chance to tell. You tell me." Olivia sighed. Aunt Lisa folded her arms. Karrington looked at her aunt. "You know too." Aunt Lisa nodded her head, acknowledging she knows. "Somebody needs to tell me now." Neither of them answered. "Does it have to do with Diedre? I thought I saw her in Mexico, then I saw her best friend. Rich said it was just a coincidence that she was there. I told him if Connie was there, Diedre was likely there. Is he sleeping with Diedre?" Still, neither of them wanted to answer. "Okay, it seems no one will answer me. There's no sense in either of you being here. I can fight this battle on my own. Thank you."

Olivia said, "Mad as you want to be, I'm not leaving. Can I make you something to eat?"

Aunt Lisa added, "I'll start dinner." She turned and walked away.

Olivia continued, "We're not trying to hurt you, Karrington. It's just best if it comes from Rich."

Karrington refused to make eye contact with her. She was visibly angry and wanted everyone to know it. Something was going on with her husband and no one would tell her. "I'm not one of those women who won't believe her husband is cheating. Tell me what I need to know." Before Olivia could answer, the sound of the garage door opening caught Karrington's attention.

Olivia said, "He's back. We'll both force him to talk."

Rich walked through the door. Karrington heard Aunt Lisa light into him about not answering

181

her calls. She stressed that she could have been calling about his wife. Rich didn't respond much except for the occasional yes ma'am. He walked into the living room. Karrington kept her eyes on the television. Rich asked Olivia, "Can you give us the room, please?"

Olivia stood up and walked past him saying, "If you don't this time, I will."

Karrington looked at Rich. Her eyes were tight. The anger had risen to its highest state. If she were a cursing person, this would be the moment she would curse him out. She knew beyond all doubt he was cheating. The man she thought had changed since high school was still the same. He sat down next to her. Karrington said, "Can you sit somewhere else, please?"

Rich obliged. He moved to the recliner closest to where Karrington was sitting. He dropped his head. "I don't know how to say this, Karrington."

"Just tell me the truth, Rich."

"I can't do this. I thought I could, but I can't. Seeing you sick like this is killing me. I thought I could be by your side, but it's a lot harder than I thought it would be. I'm young and full of life—"

"Oh, and I'm dying, so why waste it with me? Better or worse meant nothing to you, did it?"

"It did when I thought the worst would never happen. We're successful in our fields, we make mad money, I never expected to be in this position, Karrington. Having to cancel all my events and take leave for a 26-year-old wife. I never thought that would be possible for me. I just can't do it."

"It's Diedre, isn't it?"

"Diedre has nothing to do with it. The moment I saw your breasts, I knew I couldn't handle it. I'm used to perfection and—"

"You're lying. My breast may not look the same anymore, but Dr. Chase said I can have cosmetic surgery to fix most of it." Karrington gathered herself as she boiled over with fury. "Diedre was in Mexico, Rich. The same place you picked for us to go. What, you decided to kill two birds with one stone? I would be sick in the hotel while you hung out with Diedre. The arguments you've been saying were work, were Diedre, weren't they? Tell the truth." Rich didn't respond to her questions. "I knew it. I suspected you were cheating, but I didn't want to believe it." Tears flowed down her face. He tried to caress her, but she pushed him away. "Get away from me!" Olivia walked into the room.

"That's enough. Rich, you've said what you wanted to say. Get your stuff and leave my friend alone."

Rich didn't argue with her. He headed for the bedroom. Aunt Lisa joined Karrington and Olivia in the living room. Karrington cried her eyes out while they consoled her. Aunt Lisa said, "I will move in

183

here with you, baby. You took care of Momma and you have always been there for me. I will never leave you."

"Thank you, Auntie."

"You know I'll be here. When I'm not working, I will come here. Before you say something, Maurice will understand. We've already had the conversation."

"Thank you both."

Olivia hugged her as they heard the garage door open and close. "You should know that his car was not totaled, either. He gave that car to Diedre because she lost everything when her husband got caught using drugs. He's been supporting Diedre with an apartment in Northwest. The night I stayed here with you, I couldn't sleep, so I got up to get some water. I overheard something in the living room. He was video chatting with her, and she was naked on the call. When I caught him, he quickly hung up and said she was naked. I told him if he didn't tell you, I would. Then he started saying he couldn't handle you going through the sickness. I think that's bull... he wants Diedre back. That's the truth."

Karrington said, "How could I be such a fool? Why didn't I see this."

"He knew all the things to say, baby," Aunt Lisa added. "You are no fool."

"I should just give up now, so I'm not a burden to anyone else."

Olivia shot up, "Oh, that's not happening! You best believe that." She folded her arms. "We, you, me and Aunt Lisa, are going to beat this demon. That's for dang sho'."

Karrington chuckled. "I can leave it up to you to make me laugh."

8 – The Road Begins Here

Okay Lord, you're telling me to rely on you and not my husband. He wasn't the man I thought he was. I get it. I will not lose my faith. Job didn't lose his faith, neither will I. Struggle as she may, Karrington dug deep inside to climb out of her bed. Aunt Lisa took her to radiation therapy. She returned home to settle herself down and deal with the aftermath of another treatment. *My hair is thinning, but I expected that. My breast may not look the same but whomever the Lord brings my way will understand and still love me.* Aunt Lisa made them lunch while Karrington struggled in the bathroom. She didn't want Aunt Lisa to do too much. Karrington knew she was too old to help much, but she refused to leave her niece alone. *Aunt Lisa knows what love is about. Rich doesn't have a clue.* Karrington heard the door open and close. She prayed Rich hadn't returned. Karrington placed her hand on the sink to give her the leverage to get up. Before she could, a caring hand reached out and helped her rise. "Thank you, Olivia. I thought you were working today."

"I was. They let me go home to get my stuff together. I'm here to tell you they are sending me to an undisclosed location for six months."

"What? So quick?"

"Yes. Sometimes in my field it happens that way. I begged them to send someone else so I could be here with you. They won't. The military has no sympathy."

"Don't worry Olivia. I will make it. Aunt Lisa is here and if necessary, I have Marlena. She's a phone call away."

"I'm so sorry, Karrington." Tears formed in Olivia's eyes. "I want to be here with you."

"I know, but this is out of your control. You have to go."

"I should never have signed up for the Air Force. What in the world was I thinking?"

"You were thinking about the love you have for the military. This is the life, honey. Do it. God has me."

"I know He does. Every day I will be in prayer for you. Count on it." She looked at her phone for the time. "I have to go."

"Did you tell Aunt Lisa?"

"Yes. She's busy making you something to eat. I think she's happy to repay the debt to you. I'm glad you have her."

"So am I. The rest of my family doesn't seem concerned. Even the uncles I love so much."

"That happens in the time of your greatest need."

"It does. Uncle Charlie told me I was living in sin, that's why I'm sick."

"You're the story of Job for sure. That's what his wife said to him."

"That's why I laughed at him and quickly cut him out of my life. I need positivity on my road to recovery."

"Amen. I gotta run. If I get a chance to text or call, you know I will."

"Thank you for everything, Olivia."

"You're welcome."

They embraced, and Olivia rushed out of the house. Karrington held her smile until Olivia couldn't see her anymore. Once out of sight, she broke down and cried. *Lord, you've allowed the enemy to take another one of my support team away. I know you have a plan for me. No matter what I see or what I hear, I will trust you.* Karrington sat on the side of the bed. That spot became her special place. It was close enough to the bathroom and comfortable enough too for her to sit. If she wanted to lie down, she could easily do that as well.

Aunt Lisa came into the room. "Are you ready to eat, baby?"

"I don't know, I'm really not hungry, I guess I can try to eat something."

"Okay, I'll bring it in on a tray for you."

"Thank you, Aunt Lisa." Karrington wanted to lie down, but since the food would be ready soon, she stayed sitting. Aunt Lisa came back into the bedroom. "It smells good Auntie."

"I hope you enjoy it."

"I'm sure it's good." Aunt Lisa sat the tray on a stand in front of Karrington. They blessed the food and Karrington tried to eat. She looked at Aunt Lisa, who waited for an approval. Karrington wiped her mouth, "Aunt Lisa, I'm sure it's good, but I don't have an appetite right now."

"I'm sorry, baby. I'm sure it will get better soon."

Aunt Lisa pulled up a chair and ate lunch with Karrington. Karrington enjoyed the time she spent with her aunt. She learned so many things about the family's history. She loved it when Aunt Lisa lit into Uncle Charlie for saying Karrington sinned, therefore she was sick. "Aunt Lisa, I don't understand why people talk about sickness like that. Didn't Uncle Charlie read the book of Job?"

"Charlie is ignorant. Don't pay him any attention. You fight to get better, then fight even harder to stay healthy. That's what I want you to do, Karrington."

"I will, Aunt Lisa." Karrington ate all her food. It was weird for her to eat without being hungry, but she needed the nutrition. Aunt Lisa took the plates into the kitchen. Karrington laid down to get some rest. "Aunt Lisa, I'm laying down now."

"Okay, baby. Get some rest."

That I will Auntie. Karrington slept well after her meal. The side effects didn't hit her bad. When she woke, she read her texts, one of which Olivia sent. It made her smile. Olivia sent a short video telling her she was in her prayers. *No matter where she is in the world, Olivia has my back.* Karrington got up and walked into the living room. Aunt Lisa was asleep in the chair, the television watching her. Karrington touched her lightly, "Auntie."

"Hey baby, you woke up."

"Yes, Auntie." Karrington moved to the couch and took a seat. "The television always ends up watching you."

"That it does, baby. When you get my age, it will be the same for you."

"That's the part I hate about being the youngest grandchild. I bet you guys were something in your younger days. I would have loved to see that."

"Yeah, the Lewis family was something back then. Your cousins, the older ones, they got the full effect. Now everyone has drifted apart, and we rarely see each other anymore."

"That's a shame. Everyone didn't even come to grandma's funeral. I hated that."

"So did I. Are you ready to eat again?"

"No Auntie. I really don't have an appetite. Plus, it makes me run to the bathroom. These side effects are kicking my butt."

"That no good husband of yours should be here to go through this with you."

"That's on him. He'll get his reward."

"I know that's right." Aunt Lisa got up. "Well, I'm going to make something, anyway. Maybe by the time I finish, you'll be hungry."

"Okay Aunt Lisa. I can help."

"No, you can't. You're sick baby. Just relax."

Karrington didn't want to fuss with her. She actually felt good at the moment. Marlena called on Karrington's cell. "Hi Minister Sutherland. How are you?"

"Here we go with the minister thing. I'm doing well, but you sound good."

"Yes, I got a good rest."

"I heard about Rich. Darn shame."

"He says he can't handle it, so I respect that."

"He vowed to be there for better or worse."

"Marlena, no one remembers those vows when they have to keep them."

"You do."

"Well, I'm the exception." They both chuckled. "It's all good Marlena. He's with the one he really wants to be with. I think he used my condition as an excuse to leave. I think he started seeing her before I was diagnosed."

"Well, not to worry. God has you wrapped in his arms. Nothing will defeat you."

"Thank you, Marlena."

"You're welcome. I will check on you from time to time."

"Thank you."

"Have a good evening, Karrington."

"You, too." She hung up the phone. "Auntie, that was my friend Marlena. She's the minister." Aunt Lisa didn't respond. "Auntie?" Karrington shot up from the couch. She didn't know where she got the strength. Aunt Lisa sat in one of the kitchenette chairs slumped over the table. *Oh, no!* Karrington rushed to her. "Auntie! Auntie!" She pulled out her phone and called 9-1-1.

Karrington waited in the waiting room of Washington General Hospital. She sat close to the bathroom, knowing she would be in there several times. She worried about being in a place where many were sick, and her cancer weakened her immune system. But she had no other choice. No one else in the family cared enough about Aunt Lisa to be there for her. Karrington knew they would come running if

Aunt Lisa passed. They would come running for what they could get from her estate. It was the same thing they did when her grandmother passed. *I will make sure my estate is locked down so only the people I designate will get from it.*

A doctor came out. She called, "Karrington Johnson?"

Karrington hated that last name, but that was a matter for another day. She rose and met the doctor. "How's Aunt Lisa?"

"She had a stroke. It's a good thing you were around when it happened. I understand she lives alone. If you weren't there, she wouldn't have made it."

Karrington held back the flood of more tears. "Can I see her?"

"She's resting right now. Come back in the morning and see her."

"It will have to be the afternoon. I have my radiation treatment in the mornings."

The doctor nodded her head. "I see. You look strong for a woman undergoing that. Is it your breast?"

"Yes ma'am."

"I had it too. It was a struggle and I had to fight. I told my cancer if it wanted me, it was going to need to fight harder than me. It might seem like your world is ending, but honey, it's not. You can survive and ring that freaking bell as hard as you can!"

Karrington laughed. The doctor was truly inspiring. "I will do that doctor…"

"Washington, Dr. Lindsey Washington." She reached into her pocket and handed her a business card. "If you ever need to talk, I will be there. I love a good fight!"

"Amen, thank you Dr. Washington."

"Lindsey."

"Thank you, Lindsey."

"Great. Come back tomorrow afternoon. I'm sure your aunt will want to see you."

"I will do that." Karrington turned and walked away. Now she was alone… truly alone. No one was able to be with her in the house. She would have to take care of herself. *Lord, just like Job, you let me hit rock bottom. All of my support system has been taken away. I trust you.* A tear rolled down her cheek. *I trust you Jesus, I do.*

Day Three

Karrington forced herself out of the bed. The night was long and difficult for her, but she made it through. This day would be harder. No one was available to take her to her treatment. It was a gloomy day outside. The world seemed stacked against her. Karrington made it to the bathroom and got dressed.

It was a two hour struggle. The diarrhea stepped up its game on her body. She noticed that little pieces of her skin from her breast flaked off as she continued to make sense of it all. Karrington felt weaker than ever before. She made it back to the bed. Karrington slumped over and cried. *I can't do this, Lord. Just take me now. I thought I was strong… I'm not.* Karrington felt the sweet whisper of a voice in her ears. She looked around the room. With renewed strength, she made it to the kitchen where the alarm system activation box was on the wall. No one had come into the house. *Now I'm losing my mind too. Lord, I can't make it. Take me home, Jesus.*

There was the voice again. It simply said, *"Yes, you can."*

God, are you speaking to me? I don't know if you are God, but I hear you. Karrington grabbed her purse and phone. She ordered her ride share. It wasn't long before it arrived. Karrington got inside.

The driver smiled at her. "Hello, you look beautiful today."

Karrington smiled at the man, knowing his comment was just to make her feel better. "Thank you, sir. I know I look a mess."

"No, no, you are beautiful. Never let anyone tell you otherwise."

"Thank you so much." The man was jolly and lifted her spirits on the drive to the center. Karrington hoped he would pick her up on the way back.

After her treatment, she felt weak and her breast burned. Karrington tried to call Marlena to see if she was available to help her, but she didn't answer. Karrington looked to schedule another ride share when she heard the voice, "Hey girl."

"Marlena! I just tried to call you."

"My phone is on two percent. You need a ride?"

"How did you know I would be here?"

"I'm a minister, honey. They give us information. This morning I heard about Aunt Lisa and knew you would be alone. I tried to catch you before you came here, but I missed you. I wasn't going to miss giving you a ride home."

"Thank you. I need to go to the hospital to see Aunt Lisa."

"Even better. Let's do it. How was your treatment?"

"Horrible. I'm weak. I have diarrhea off and on and I don't have an appetite. Do you know what that means for a foodie?"

"The struggle is real, honey."

"Marlena, can I confide in you?"

"Of course."

"This morning I gave up. I told God he could call me home. I told him that I couldn't do this."

"You know that's normal. At some point, most of us in your position would have that moment. But you didn't give up. You got yourself to your treatment, and you got through it. Now you're on your way to see your aunt. Your family is filled with healthy people who won't go see your aunt."

"I know that's right."

"You'll be fine, honey. Next time call me… please."

"I will Marlena." Karrington paused then said, "I heard a voice say 'Yes you can' after I said I couldn't do it anymore. I thought someone was in my house. I looked around and checked the alarm, but no one was there." She looked at Marlena. "Then I heard the voice again. Was it God?"

"I would put my last dollar on it. God is allowing these things to happen to you, but your faith will carry you through Karrington. You are strong. I've always noticed that about you. This too… will pass."

"I hope you're right. I can't feel much lower than I do right now." Marlena looked at her. "My husband left me, my best friend got called away to an undisclosed location, my aunt had a stroke; last night I was alone, and it hurt." She cried.

197

"Don't cry Karrington. You should have called me. I would have been here."

"You have a family of your own. I couldn't pull you away from them."

"Look, my husband is very understanding. We went through cancer with his sister. If I told him you needed me, he would be fine with it. I'm staying with you tonight." Before Karrington could reply, Marlena said, "If you're about to say no or something like that, save it. I'm staying."

Karrington smiled, knowing she would not win that argument. They pulled up to the hospital. Karrington went in to see Aunt Lisa. Some of her brothers and sisters finally made it to see her. That was good. Karrington hoped they would. She got to spend 30 minutes with her, and Marlena prayed over her. Afterwards, they left. Marlena picked up some clothes from her home and returned with Karrington.

The Struggle Continues

Each day was a challenge for Karrington. Most days Marlena could be with her, but there were days when she couldn't. Throw in Karrington's support for Aunt Lisa and times were very difficult for her. She was one week away from finishing her treatment. During this time, Karrington returned to work amid threats of firing her. She arrived after her treatment and sat at her desk. Karrington had a new secretary that was hired while she was out. Susie

Means walked into Karrington's office. "Good morning, ma'am. My name is Susie. I'm your new secretary."

"Hi Susie. It's good to meet you."

"For the record, I think it's wrong of them to put you on notice like that. You won a big high-profile case for them. They should understand what you're going through."

"They're men. It's to be expected, Susie. I'm able to resume my work. It's not ideal for me, but nothing will stop me from ringing that bell next week."

"May I sit down?"

"Of course."

"My mom went through breast cancer." Susie's face tightens, her lips quivered. "She didn't win. I understand your battle and I hope you win it. My mom didn't get to ring that bell. There's not a day that goes by that I don't feel her presence. When they offered me this job and I was told about your battle, I knew this would be the job for me."

"Thank you, Susie. I'm sorry for your loss. I lost a grandmother to cancer. My mother battled it and won, but then died in a car accident. It's like fate comes for the Lewis women."

Susie replied, "Well, fate won't get you. I'll be praying for you."

"Thank you."

"Anything you need me to do?"

"Well, we need to get to work on the Cardington case. He's charged with rape."

"Ewe."

"Yeah, I know, but we're a defense firm, so we have to work with all kinds."

"Yes ma'am. I'll pull his file."

Susie walked out of the office, leaving Karrington with her thoughts. She hated defending rapists and murderers, too. The thought of opening her own firm dwelled in her mind. The partners in her firm were understanding at first. Now they threatened to fire her if she didn't return to work sick or not. She thought, *I can open a firm designed to help women keep their rights. There's no reason for them to fire me. I would be returning to work next week. I believe they wanted this office for someone else and I was an easy target. I'm not going to give it to them.* Her desk intercom rang. "This is Karrington."

"Hi ma'am, there's a call for you on line six."

"Thank you, Susie." She clicked over to line six, "This is Karrington Lewis. How may I help you?"

"Karrington, how are you?"

"How am I? I'm doing well Rich; not that it matters much to you."

"It matters to me, honey."

"Don't call me that."

"You're still my wife." Karrington didn't respond. "Anyway, I wanted to give you a heads up." Karrington looked up, and a man stood at her doorway. She held up a finger, telling him to wait.

"For what Rich?"

"I filed for divorce. They will serve you soon."

Karrington looked at the man. He wore a suit and professional glasses. To her, he looked the server type. She motioned for him to come in. "Hold on Rich." She asked the man, "What do you have for me?"

"Are you Karrington Johnson?"

"Yes. Hand it to me."

The man handed her the envelope. "You've been served Miss Johnson."

He turned and walked out of the office. She returned to her call with Rich. "Your timing is impeccable. The man was just here to serve me." She glanced over at the documents.

"I'm sorry, Karrington. I never imagined being in this situation with you. You seemed so healthy—"

"Stop right there, Rich. You're using my medical issues as an excuse. I know you were seeing Diedre before my issues. Stop lying."

"Okay, if you want the truth, yes, I was. Diedre knows how to treat me in bed and out. You just didn't have it. I imagined it so better—"

Karrington hung up the phone and continued reading the documents. She was appalled at them. She made a call. "Hey Marlena, can you meet for dinner tonight?"

"I sure can. What time honey?"

"Six at Estelle's on First Street."

"I will be there. How are you feeling?"

"I am doing well. I can see myself ringing that bell next week."

"Outstanding! How's Aunt Lisa?"

"Adjusting. At least one of my cousins moved in with her to help. That was good because I was just too sick to do it. I check on her every day to make sure they're good."

"That's great. I've had both of you in my prayers and it appears God is answering them."

"Yes, He is. Thank you and I'll see you tonight."

"Yes, you will. Bye now."

"Bye Marlena."

Karrington and Susie worked closely through the afternoon. She gathered her things and headed to Estelle's for dinner with Marlena. Once seated at the table she reviewed the menu and decided on a Cobb salad. Marlena arrived shortly afterwards, and they ordered dinner. Marlena said, "You're going for the salad?"

"Yes ma'am, I'm intent on staying with eating healthy and exercising. I'm getting stronger, so I make sure I walk a mile a day to start. The stronger I get, the more I will walk."

"Sounds like the worst is behind you."

"You just don't know how hard it was for me. Losing my support system and today, Mr. Johnson served me with divorce papers."

"What? The nerve of that guy."

"Tell me about it. He wants the house, too."

"I hope you're fighting that."

"I started to. That was my initial reaction, but now I think I'll let him buy me out. I want a new home, somewhere he's not been. A new start to my life."

"Love it Karrington." They toasted to Karrington's new start. "What about those jerks at work?"

"I'm not doing anything about them right now. After next week and after my divorce, I plan to open my own firm. I want to represent women. Not every woman is as fortunate as I have been. Had it not been for my job and winning that big case, I wouldn't have the funds to start over. I'm sure there are many women who can't do that. I want to help them."

"Again, I love it."

"It won't be as lucrative, but hey, I feel God is leading me in that direction."

Marlena said, "Hey, once you're ready, start one of the fundraising platforms. You never know how many people will give to help you start your firm."

"Good idea. I'll do that."

9 – Ring That Bell!

Karrington waited for Dr. Chase to join her in the examination room. The last month rolled through her mind. *Wow, I've been diagnosed with cancer, lost my husband, my best friend was sent somewhere in the world, my favorite aunt had a stroke but I'm still here. Praise God. Who says faith doesn't reward the faithful? I feel better than I have ever felt in my life. I don't know if my body adjusted to the treatment or not. Something inside me feels different.*

Dr. Chase walked into the room. "Hello Miss Johnson."

"Please don't call me by that name. I'm Karrington Lewis."

"Alright. I'm guessing there's trouble in paradise."

"He left me at the beginning of my treatment. So I'm going to complete it without him."

"Unfortunately, this is not the first time I have heard that story. Men don't understand what our bodies go through and when we have to fight for our survival, some of them can't handle it. I'm sorry he left you."

"I'm not. I learned that I should have gone with my initial gut feeling. He hasn't changed since high school. In the beginning, he made me believe he did. He used my illness as an excuse to leave me. I believe if I didn't have cancer, he would have left me, anyway. He never stopped loving his first love."

"I see. He had issues on several levels." They each chuckled. "I usually don't say this. I had a bad feeling when he came in here. I wasn't feeling him."

"Same feeling I probably had in the beginning. I think I fell for the opportunities his contacts gave me. Through him I got the job in the law firm I work in. Now they want to fire me because I was sick."

"Wow, you are facing trouble on many sides. Have you talked to the doctor I gave you?"

"No, I've been talking to a minister. She's been awesome. She also stayed at my house when I had no one else to stay with me. I couldn't have done it without her."

"That's amazing Karrington. Now let me have a look at you." Dr. Chase examined Karrington. She hated the examination, but she knew it was necessary. "Hmm, aside from the surgical areas, you look good. I'm impressed with your healing."

"It's God, not me."

"Amen to that." Dr. Chase wrote her notes on the computer. "When is your last treatment?"

"Thursday."

"Good. I want to be there when you ring that bell."

"I would be glad to have you. I'm videotaping it, so my best friend will get to see it. She's somewhere in the world. The Air Force sent her away, and I want to make sure she gets an opportunity to view it."

"That's a great idea. I will schedule your follow up for Friday. We'll draw some blood and see where we stand. If we have to do another biopsy, we'll schedule that for next week."

"Okay, Dr. Chase."

"Well, I'm all done here. Any questions for me?"

"Nope. I'm good."

"That's great. Have a great day Karrington."

"You too, Dr. Chase." Karrington headed out of the office. She felt good about her examination. Now she needed to go talk to the partners at her law firm. They scheduled a meeting for her, two days before she would ring the bell. She knew they wanted to get rid of her. Karrington also learned from her previous secretary that they were firing her because of Rich. He was evil.

Karrington pulled up at the firm and marched inside. She would not allow herself to be defeated by anyone. God had her back, and she would not bow down to anyone else. Karrington walked through the big double doors like she owned them. Susie quickly met her. "They have been waiting for you in the conference room."

"Not to worry Susie. I got this."

"Good."

Karrington walked into the conference room. The partners consisted of six men and two women. It disgusted Karrington that the women would take part in this atrocity. She took a seat in front of them. Guy spoke up, "Karrington… we'll get right to the point. You're a great attorney and your win in the Tyre case helped this firm's reputation a great deal. However, your recent illness costs this firm money and frankly, we can't continue down this road. We're prepared to offer you a gracious severance package." He slid the document across the table to Karrington.

Karrington picked it up and skimmed over it. "We all know this isn't about my sickness. It's about my husband—"

"Your husband has nothing to do with this," insisted Guy. "He's not part of this firm."

"No, but he's part of your club."

"Karrington—"

"Stop Guy, just stop the nonsense. I'm prepared to take this package. However, you need to add another year of pay on here."

One partner shouted, "That's ridiculous. We are already being generous to you."

"Then we'll be in court. We all know I'll win the moment I bring up my illness. You want to please my husband, add a year to the package and I'll accept it."

The managing partner chimed in, "Add it." He rose from the table and marched out.

Karrington smirked at the rest of them. They all knew she had won. She was an excellent attorney, and she would make them sorry they let her go. One by one they all left, leaving Guy and Karrington alone. "Just between me and you, Karrington. I didn't want this."

"It doesn't matter Guy. I'm getting a lot of money to start my own firm. I'm okay with it."

"Be careful Karrington." He stood up to walk out. "Rich will come after this money."

"Let him."

"I'll amend the package and bring it to your office."

"Thanks, Guy." Karrington remained in the seat for a few minutes, proud of the woman she had become. Everything the enemy attacked her with failed. Now she needed to ring that bell and divorce her husband. She stood and returned to her office. Susie joined her. "Susie, I took the severance package."

"No."

"Don't worry. Lay low here. Once I start my firm, you can come work for me."

"I'd love that, Miss Lewis."

"Awesome. I'll pack up my stuff."

"I'll help you."

"Thank you."

Karrington sat in her living room, watching the latest news on television. She smiled when the report came that Micah Hill was re-signed by Seattle, giving him another chance at professional football. During the interview, Diedre stood by him. *I wonder what she did with Rich this time. I know one thing, he's not coming back here.* She poured herself a glass of water and made one of her now famous salads. Eating healthy was once hard, but now she has adopted the habit. Karrington was determined to give her body every opportunity to heal.

Later that evening, she prepared for bed. Karrington got on her knees and prayed, *God, my last month has been a difficult one. I know you have been there. I felt your presence in the beginning and throughout my journey. On Thursday, I will ring that bell. Everyone will see it as a testament that I completed my treatment. Truthfully, it's a testament of my faith in You. Thank you, Lord, for all you have done, will do and are doing on my behalf. I love you, Lord, today, right now, and tomorrow. In your wonderful Son Jesus' name… Amen.*

The Day Arrived

Thursday morning couldn't have been more beautiful for Karrington. It's true the rain poured down over the district., but to Karrington, it was a beautiful day. She dressed and headed to the clinic for her last treatment. Afterwards she would ring the bell, signifying her completion of her radiation therapy. Just as she did at the law firm on her last day, she burst through the clinic doors, ready to take the last treatment by storm. She walked inside and the tech set her up as usual. He mentioned that Dr. Chase had an emergency and couldn't' be there but would see her tomorrow. Twenty minutes later, the treatment was completed. The bell she'd passed so many times waited for her in the hallway. On day one, it looked so intimidating, like something she would never get to do. Now, the bell looked small, easy to strike a blow at. The tech agreed to film the moment for Karrington. She didn't wait for any dramatic moment. Karrington walked up to the bell and rang it with all her might. She remembered what the doctor said to her after Aunt Lisa had her stroke; Karrington remembered her husband's words when he left her; she remembered the sad moment of watching her best friend leave; she remembered the partners at her firm firing her because of Rich; all those things went into striking that bell.

Karrington jumped for joy. She clasped her hands and thanked God for all he had done.

Follow Up Results

Karrington enjoyed a weekend spa trip in New York City with Marlena. Monday arrived faster than anyone wanted. Karrington wanted to know her results. She continued to feel good. The hope that all of this was behind her dwelled within her. Dr. Chase walked into the room. "Karrington, how are you doing?"

"I am doing really well, Dr. Chase."

"You should."

"Why do you say that?"

"There's nothing in your blood work that says you have cancer… nothing. That also means no chemo either."

"Thank you, Jesus!"

"I thought there would be a trace, but this is the best result we could have hoped for."

"I feel so good, Dr. Chase."

"Whatever you're doing, keep doing it."

Karrington stood up, "It's called prayer with faith. Thank you, Dr. Chase." Karrington walked out, loving her life. She arrived on the street to get her car; she spotted Rich standing by it. He smiled, but she wasn't having it. "Hello Rich. I'm surprised to see you here. Oh, but wait. Didn't I see Diedre with Micah?"

"I want to come home, Karrington."

Karrington's first thought was to be as mean as she could to him. She knew that wouldn't be the Godly way. Instead, she said, "Rich, there is no place for us anymore. You made it clear where you stand and how you feel about me. Now, please step aside so I can get in my car."

Rich appeared to make a comeback statement. However, she moved to the side. Karrington got into her car, let the top down, and drove off with a big smile pasted on her face.

10 – Six Months Later

Karrington stood in front of the building she leased for her new office. Susie waved from inside, happy to start her new position with Karrington's new firm. Olivia and Marlena walked up from behind. Olivia said, "I'm proud of you, Karrington. You went down to rock bottom but made it all the way back and then some."

"I couldn't have done it without the two of you and Aunt Lisa."

Marlena added, "Don't forget God."

"How can I forget Him? Without Him at the head of my life, I would be nothing."

Olivia asked, "How's Aunt Lisa?"

"Good. She hasn't had another stroke since. She's able to move around and everything."

Marlena asked, "And Rich? Have you heard from him?"

"Well, it seems his partners turned on him when they saw how I bounced back. He lost his job. Last I heard, he was out of work. I drove by the house and it's up for sale now. I haven't seen him lately. I don't know how he's doing. All I know is I'm a single woman again. I have my health, my own firm, money in the bank, good friends, and family."

Both Marlena and Olivia said, "Amen."

"Let's go inside and have some coffee in my new office." They all walked inside and enjoyed a cup of coffee and girl talk. The next weekend, Olivia and Maurice would get married. Karrington was the maid of honor. She prayed Olivia's marriage would do better than her marriage did.